Coping with Emotional Disorders

Carolyn Simpson and Dwain Simpson

THE ROSEN PUBLISHING GROUP, INC./NEW YORK

Published in 1991 by The Rosen Publishing Group, Inc.
29 East 21st Street, New York, NY 10010

First Edition

Manufactured in the United States of America

Library of Congress Cataloging-in-Publication Data

Simpson, Carolyn.
Coping with emotional disorders / Carolyn Simpson with Dwain Simpson.—1st ed.
p. cm.—(Coping)
Includes bibliographical references.
Includes index.
Summary: Discusses emotional disorders, how to deal with your own and those of a family member, and where to go for help.
ISBN 0-8239-1238-8
1. Mental illness—Juvenile literature. 2. Psychiatric hospital care—Juvenile literature. [1. Mental illness.] I. Simpson. Dwain, 1951- . II. Title. III. Series.
RC460.2.S54 1991
616.89—dc20

90-47998
CIP
AC

Manufactured in the United States of America

ABOUT THE AUTHORS ◇

Carolyn Simpson is currently a teacher/counselor in an alternative education program at Lake Region High School in western Maine. She holds a Master's Degree in Human Relations and has worked for twelve years in the field of mental health—nine of those years as a clinical social worker. In addition to her counseling experience, she has taught sociology and human relations courses at Oscar Rose Junior College in Midwest City, Oklahoma. She is the author of another book in this series, *Coping with an Unplanned Pregnancy* (1990) and numerous children's picture books.

Dwain Simpson is a licensed clinical social worker who works at Western Maine Counseling Service in Bridgton, Maine, and has a private practice in Portland. He holds an MSW (as well as a degree in Political Science) from the University of Oklahoma and has been a social worker for the past thirteen years. In his off-hours he tries to squeeze in an occasional half-marathon, although he has been known to run shorter distances competitively (and to exercise the dog.)

He and his wife met in a mental institution in Oklahoma, so they know that good things can happen there. They are the parents of three wild and woolly preadolescents, not to mention caretakers of a dog and a cat.

Acknowledgments

Aside from the books we used as background for this book, our story would not have been so complete without the help of our friends and colleagues who shared their experiences with us.

Our thanks go to Greg Carbone, PhD, a psychologist in private practice and Director of Psychological Testing Services at Jackson Brook Institute, South Portland, Maine; Troy Clark, MSW/LCSW, a clinician on the Adolescent Unit of Jackson Brook Institute; H. Rollin Ives, EdD, Maine State Commissioner of Human Services; Linda Hertell of the Maine State Bureau of Mental Health; Stuart Garrison, PhD, Clinical Director of Western Maine Counseling Service, Bridgton; and Dr. Robert Allanach, Executive Director of Western Maine Institute for Psychotherapy and Education, Bridgton. Thanks, too, to our longtime friends and colleagues: Sondra Shehab, MSW/LCSW, a private psychotherapist in Norman, Oklahoma, and Sallie Clote, Director of Social Services at Norman Regional Hospital; to Joyce Doherty Cotton, RN, MEd, CS, and Richard O'Toole, LCSW, clinicians at Western Maine Counseling Service; Michael Kramer, PhD, a psychologist in private practice in Portland, Maine; and my good friend (and budding photographer) Marcia Goodwin of Norman, Oklahoma.

As with my other book, our clients (past and present) have helped shape these pages, offering their personal stories and triumphs. Special thanks to them (though all identifying attributes have been altered to ensure privacy) and to my students: Stacy, Leah, Regina, Kelly, Jennifer, Missy, and Trena.

With gratitude and love to our kids—Michal, Jaime, and Jarrett—who ate more than their share of peanut butter sandwiches while we worked on this book.

Lastly, because of all the landlord hassles we suffered during the time we wrote this book, we can honestly say: Bad things *do* happen to good people...

A WORD ABOUT THE WRITING OF THIS BOOK

Writing this book from a "we" point of view raised too many problems. It added a confusing dimension to our stories and philosophies (since we don't agree on everything), and it would have made the book less personal.

Because of that (and because Dwain does not like to write outside of psychosocial evaluations), I have written the narrative, utilizing my own interviews and Dwain's, plus many pages of his advice. Where the stories or experiences are mine, they are so indicated, and Dwain's contributions are similarly acknowledged.

Carolyn Simpson
June 1990

Contents

Preface

No doubt you have heard stories about kids living with "crazy" relatives. Maybe you live with one or two yourself. Either mothers or fathers who can't get themselves out of bed in the morning—or by dinnertime, for that matter. Or older siblings, aunts or uncles who spend the greater part of the day staring at the walls, unable to connect with anyone else in the family.

Perhaps you have a brother or sister who is locked away in a hospital or group home because he or she is unable to behave up to society's expectations. Yet despite your sibling's being the one branded a problem, he or she is the focus of family attention and energy. Which leaves you—the normal child—WHERE?

It is downright maddening to live in a household where a member has some form of emotional disturbance. It's scary, too, because the people you care about are not behaving as you would normally expect. Childhood and adolescence are times when you especially need those around you to be stable, predictable, and normal. After all, the times themselves are turbulent enough!

It is strange, too, to be in this kind of household because you probably don't know how to act around your relatives anymore or how to help them get back to acting normal. How do you bring your friends into a crazy, unpredictable household like yours?

But what if the person in your family struggling with an

emotional disturbance is YOU? How do you signal others for help, and what kind of help is out there for you?

Those are the very questions we hope to answer for you in this book.

It is important to understand that not all emotional upsets lead to a bona fide illness. In this book we shall cover the various disturbances, including the more transitory (nonlasting) conditions as well as more severe forms of mental illness. For example, many teens admit feeling depressed, but when the clinician uses the term depressed he or she may mean something far more serious.

You may be feeling "down" because things haven't gone right today, but some people are "permanently down"—so far that they lose interest in the world and even in life. Depression, like the other forms of mood disorders we shall describe, is often a matter of degree. Thus it is important to understand when a mere mood has become a serious disorder—and what to do about it.

At the point where you need outside intervention and/or supervision (either because you can't think straight or don't want to think straight), this book will help give you a perspective on your situation. Or on the situation of those you care about, who may be going through these problems.

We've divided this book into two parts. First, we'll consider the other person having the emotional disturbance. We'll describe the major forms of illness in words that you can understand, and we'll suggest ways of coping with their symptoms and the often stigmatizing way society looks upon you all afterwards.

The second and larger section of our book will deal with you as the person experiencing the emotional disturbance. As we mentioned earlier, emotional disorders can manifest themselves by degree, so some types of upsets can be managed with outpatient counseling while others respond better to hospitalization and a much more structured environment. Admissions to adolescent psychiatric units have been on the rise nationally. Are emotional disturbances truly on the increase, or are hospitals becoming dumping grounds for kids whose parents can no longer control them? You should know the difference.

We think the better informed you are (no matter what your age), the less traumatic these experiences can be for you. It is toward this end—educating you about your options for treatment and pointing you toward restored health—that we write this book.

Lastly, it is no crime to be subject to the whims of your emotions. But at the same time, it's certainly no picnic. We hope that this book and its stories will show you ways of *Coping With Emotional Disorders*, whether they're your own or another family member's. . . .

PART ◇ I

UNDERSTANDING MENTAL ILLNESS IN YOUR FAMILY

CHAPTER ◇ 1

Understanding What Is Happening

Many years ago when I was a social worker on the geriatric ward of a state hospital, I took a shine to a man who was a senile patient. George Henderly was sixty-five as near as we could tell. He had a thick mass of white hair that he never bothered to comb. He had no idea what his name was, where he was, or even what century it was. But for all his ramblings and confusion, he had a great sense of humor. It was as if he thought his predicament (a mind that had run away from him) was amusing, and therefore he took pleasure in whatever he recalled or recognized. No family ever visited George. So there he was everyday, watching a blank television screen or wandering through the activities rooms, muttering suggestive remarks to women and occasionally flashing himself through his unbuttoned, state-issued clothing.

One day I decided to free George—temporarily, anyway. A male aide and I signed George out for a few hours' pass. We took him to the duck pond, the most social spot in Norman, Oklahoma, at the time. George rode happily in the car, though he must have been even more confused than usual to have left his familiar ward. The aide and I kept up what we thought was a lively conversation; George merely smiled and fingered his pants.

I didn't start worrying that George would do something inappropriate until we got out of the car and saw all the families playing together around the duck pond. George walked woodenly past all the ducks and barking dogs. The aide and I flanked him and tried to anticipate anything rude he might suddenly do or say. We sat down on the grass and pointed out all the neat things there—the blue sky, the kids chasing the ducks, the bugs crawling through the grass, the smell of barbecue wafting on the wind. But George was locked in his own private world and just kept smiling.

"What are you thinking about?" I asked him.

"I've got to go to the bathroom," he said.

Well, that was the end of our trip into the free world. Knowing that George had a habit of urinating behind desks and doorways, we hurried him back to the hospital so that he wouldn't expose himself in the park. He shuffled back onto the ward as if nothing unusual had happened.

I mention this incident because some of you may have had to deal with a similarly confused older relative. George was a warm human being, and I could delight (at times) in his company; but I didn't have to live with George, and when things got touchy I could bring him right back to the hospital. I didn't have to deal with his illness and deterioration every day of my life; furthermore, I didn't have to take his problems personally. How much more difficult it would have been had he been my father or a beloved uncle. Not only would I have grieved for his embarrassment (and mine), but I might have worried that his illness foreshadowed a similar fate for me, since we were related.

Perhaps this is a good time to discuss the various types of illness you might encounter: the symptoms and the chances for cure or management. In a later chapter I'll talk about how you might fit into all of this.

ANXIETY

I once had a roommate in college who was nervous about taking a final exam. She studied for weeks before that test, although she was an honors student who had no cause to be worried. Nonetheless, she made herself physically sick over the test, and as she took her seat in the examining room she quite literally got sick. She tore out of the room, heaved up her guts in the bathroom, and then returned to the examining room, completed the test, and earned an honors grade. That was *anxiety*.

Everyone from time to time gets nervous about things, especially things beyond our control. Anxiety signals the body that something is wrong or out of the ordinary. Our response, complete with the surge of adrenalin, helps us deal with the event or circumstance. I'm not talking about that kind of anxiety here, because that is something we all live with in varying amounts, and it is actually beneficial. But beyond the everyday kind of anxiety are the pervasive, incapacitating anxiety attacks, often called panic attacks.

If you know someone who suffers from chronic severe anxiety, you might think he or she is faking it. After all, we all live with anxiety; these are anxious times. Can't a person just will him or herself to calm down?

Let me give you an example of a woman I have known for ten years. Marcia suffers from severe anxiety, and although it is manageable with medication, it still prevents her from living a full life. When Marcia first came to see me, getting to her appointments was a major ordeal. Many were the times when she had to pull over on the side of the road to vomit because she was so anxious just being out in public. Sometimes she couldn't do her grocery shopping on the way home because she was too paralyzed with anxiety to get out of the car. Unpredictable attacks of diarrhea further complicated her life, making public appearances hazardous to her dignity. Not many people believed in her panic attacks—even some doctors who examined her when she applied for disability payments. "If you can make it into town for appointments," they typically said, "you can make it into town to work. You just are using your anxiety as a crutch."

Even *they* assumed that she could overcome her immobility, brought on by the excruciating physical symptoms of anxiety—the heart flutterings, the dizziness, the ice-cold panic that swept through her body, making her unable to lift her feet off the ground. Those alternated with unrelenting bouts of diarrhea and vomiting.

Marcia is much better these days. Medication has made her illness a little more manageable; but more significantly, she has learned how to live with it—how to compensate for her trepidations and how to lie low when the feelings sweep over her. In fact, she has made so much progress that doctors have decided that she doesn't suffer from acute anxiety after all.

According to Dr. David Sheehan's book *The Anxiety Disease*, people pass through several stages of anxiety on their way to total incapacitation, and maybe not in this order. First are panic attacks, when the body goes haywire—pounding heart, light-headedness, that "scared" feeling: a sensation that you're going to die if you don't get out of there *right now!* In another stage a person comes to feel that he or she has symptoms of every major terminal disease there is. When I was in high school I started having "swallowing" problems before standing up in front of the class to give a speech. I would be sitting there waiting for my turn before the executioner (my sophomore English teacher), and all of a sudden my throat would shut down. I couldn't swallow the saliva that was accumulating. I would discreetly clutch at my throat, trying to push the spit down. And when I still couldn't swallow I would get scared because it felt as if I couldn't breathe either. That "temporary problem" saved me from a lot of English speeches, but it caused me much anguish. My parents thought I had troublesome tonsils at the time, but I was sure I had lockjaw and was in the stages just prior to death.

I survived lockjaw to acquire a new disease in college. One day I discovered blood in my stool, and I just knew I was dying of colon cancer. I listened to the girls making small talk in the dorm bathroom, and I thought: "These will probably be the last conversations I'll ever hear." Well, I survived hemorrhoids and went on to suffer a heart attack in my junior year. One day my whole left side tingled—you know, the side nearest your heart, the one doctors worry about when someone's left arm hurts. I rushed myself to a specialist in circulation problems, only to learn that I had "bad nerves." And a good, strong heart. Every time a diagnosis was made that suggested a problem with anxiety, I got over that symptom and went on to develop a new one.

During my Master's studies I developed unpredictable bouts of diarrhea. Doctors called it "irritable bowel syndrome," but I secretly thought I had a recurrence of the cancer I had begun in undergraduate school. I was so afraid I would have an attack during my oral examination for the degree that I took some of a friend's Valium in the hope of calming my insides. Unfortunately, I misjudged the dosage and put myself into a stupor. My professors asked me if I were stoned, which did not help me in passing that exam.

Another stage of anxiety is the phobic stage. People *feel* their anxiety about something and then associate it with their present circumstances. They start fearing crowds because they experienced that overwhelming anxiety in a crowd. The anxiety may have come from nowhere, but because it occurred in that situation, the person interprets it as a response to that situation. All kinds of avoidances can spring from this reasoning; people start avoiding more and more in an effort to keep a lid on their anxiety. Other symptoms that follow are components of depression—inertia, hopelessness, and feelings of worthlessness—nevertheless tied in to the inability to manage the anxiety.

It is important to remember that *it is not a matter of using willpower to manage this illness*. In many cases doctors have found that antidepressants or antianxiety pills have some effect on controlling the panic attacks. Because these generalized attacks may spring from a mysterious malfunction (imbalance?) in the brain, medications are often helpful.

Although it is not within the scope of this book to discuss all the drugs, briefly these are the kinds often used. The monoamine oxidase inhibitors (MAO inhibitors) and the tricyclics belong to the family of antidepressants. Benzodiazepine and diazepam are antianxiety medications and are addictive if not managed properly. Prozac has been used with varying degrees of success, mostly to combat the depressive components of the illness. As with all medications, some seem to work better than others. The antianxiety pills bring quicker relief than the antidepressants, which need to build up to a therapeutic level in the blood —sometimes eight weeks or so. But the antianxiety drugs *can* (not necessarily *will*) lead to abuse and dependence.

When a person is diagnosed as having an anxiety disorder, according to Dr. Sheehan, there are four targets of treatment:

1. Control the physical symptoms of the disease; that is, the part that can respond to medicine. No one sufficiently understands why certain chemicals alter the brain's functioning, either improving its functioning or worsening the symptoms. People only make logical guesses based on their understanding of neurotransmitters in the brain.
2. Deal with the phobias. Obviously, by the time a therapist gets to make a diagnosis of severe anxiety, there has been plenty of time for the person to develop phobias. Specific behavioral therapy, and sometimes psychotherapy, work toward that end.
3. Deal with the psychosocial stress engendered by many years of living with an anxiety condition. That means supportive counseling to counteract years of living under the threat of another panic attack.
4. Manage the anxiety to minimize possibility of relapse. Often, a trusting relationship with a therapist can go a long way toward keeping the condition under control. Both patient and therapist may see signs of relapse before they become overwhelming.

OBSESSIVE-COMPULSIVE DISORDER

The person who has to go back to check the front door fifty times before he can get in the car and drive off on a business trip may not be suffering from anxiety. Instead, he may be suffering from obsessive-compulsive disorder. If you can imagine having to check and recheck something and being unable to carry on your other activities until you have done the checking, you have a glimpse of what OCD is like. The thing to remember is that a person with OCD is *not able to keep from doing the obsessive action or thinking the repetitive thought.* It is as if the person has lost the ability to trust his or her senses. Obsessive-compulsives often get stuck in doorways, as funny as that may sound, because they simply can't get through the doorway without first performing some elaborate ritual such as touching different parts of the doorway with certain fingers. It is not a matter of saying to the person, "Oh, come on. Just walk through and let's go." The person feels compelled to go through with the ritual because not to do it brings on overwhelming anxiety.

Whenever my husband and I are traveling and know we'll be away from home for a while, one of us inevitably wants to go back after about a mile to make sure we shut off the stove or locked the front door. We thus end up minutes behind schedule, and once we start the checking there seem to be more things to check. But eventually one of us comes to his senses and tells the other to cut it out and get back in the car. For the person with OCD, it is not that simple. He or she cannot be content with just one or two checks. At the time he may be appeased, but within minutes he is unsure whether he really shut off the stove burner or turned it one digit beyond OFF—to HIGH, for instance. And that goes on and on and on. The point to remember about obsessive-compulsive disorder is that it wreaks havoc on the person's life—and on the people who live with him.

If you have a parent or sibling with this problem, you already know the exasperation of wanting to live a normal life around someone who repetitively thinks horrible thoughts or ritualizes every minute of the day.

According to Dr. Judith Rapoport's book *The Boy Who Couldn't Stop Washing*, there are more than four million sufferers of OCD in the United States alone, and "most keep their disease hidden." Imagine the isolation required to allow a person to keep these rituals secret. Imagine how many other people have labeled these sufferers simply "crazy."

People with OCD practice many types of rituals. Hand-washing (even after the hands are bloodied from repeated washings), stringing (playing with strings for hours at a time to the exclusion of any other activity), entranceway rites, and checking are the most common. Other people torture themselves with repetitive thoughts, usually bad thoughts; they cannot make it through a day without devising elaborate schemes to push the thoughts aside temporarily. Others count things: the times people have said certain words, anything at all. What all these people have in common is that they ultimately doubt themselves—their senses—because their senses tell them that something needs to be done over and over and over again.

Originally behavioral therapy was used to treat these people, but it was routinely unsuccessful. Certain medications, however, have almost totally eradicated the behaviors, which leads some doctors to conclude that OCD is a product of a brain dysfunction. Medications that are successful are invariably of two groups: either imipramine (under the trade name Tofranil), which is a tricyclic antidepressant, or Prozac, which has recently come into favor for treating depression. Reportedly, the best medication yet is Anafranil, which was expected to be available in the United States in 1990. When these drugs are successful, they enable the patient to break the cycle of endless rituals. It is almost as if the medicine allows the brain once again to recognize when certain actions have been completed.

DEPRESSION

Joshua Stone, a man in his seventies who had attempted suicide, was my patient in 1986. His presenting problem was severe depression related to a history of poor health, something that if anything would only get worse with age. In our numerous individual and family sessions I was struck by this man's pain, both physical and psychic. He wanted to end his life with dignity rather than drag out his suffering and subject his wife and children to the care of a chronically ill man. In working with his wife, I saw that she was not ready to let him go. They had been married over fifty years, and ill or not, she wanted him to stay with her. She wanted everything done to alleviate his depressive symptoms, especially his suicidal thinking.

Mr. Stone remained on our unit for several weeks, and his mood did brighten in response to medicine. But I wasn't certain that in time he wouldn't try to kill himself again. He simply didn't have the will to live, as much as his wife demanded that he do so. Within a few months of discharge, Mr. Stone died of complications from chronic emphysema.

When assessing a person for admission, we look for two types of depression. Acute episodes of depression, sometimes of the magnitude of full-blown major depression, are usually related to an event—a death, perhaps, or a loss. The other type of depression is of a more long-standing nature and seems to come from within the person. Have you ever known someone who seemed "down" from the moment you met him or her?

Both types of depression can have the same symptoms: the persistent low mood, the tearfulness, the hopelessness and negativism. Some people, rather than seeming down, appear "dead"—their emotions so repressed that they can show neither happiness nor anger. Depressed people quite often have suicidal thoughts but not necessarily the energy to act on them. Their thinking may be slowed or confused, and their judgment impaired. Some lose their appetite, whereas others gain weight. Most experience sleep disturbance, a loss of pleasure in life, called anhedonia, and lack of interest in their appearance.

An impossible task for therapists is to know when a person really means to kill himself. The most we can do is guess at the degree of a person's despair and whether he or she has the energy or capacity to carry out such an action. I suspect that every therapist has been wrong at least once, because statistically 12 out of 100,000 Americans commit suicide each year.

What causes depression? The easiest causes to spot are the external life events—the losses. In Joshua Stone's case it was the loss of his health and ultimately his independence. With others it might be the death of a loved one, a divorce, or the loss of a job and the security that conveys. People typically go through stages of grief over a loss—from numbness and shock to denial that anything bad really happened, to anger (Why me?), to bargaining (I'll go to church every Sunday the rest of my life if you'll just bring back my husband), to sadness and longing for the loved one's return, to eventual acceptance of the permanence of the loss. Some people get stuck in one of the stages of grief, quite often sadness or anger. If they cannot work through that stage, they remain with unresolved grief and depression.

With other people, there is no obvious loss. Their sadness seems to well up from within. Doctors have postulated that a chemical imbalance is reponsible for their depression and that it may be genetically linked, so that more than one person in a family may develop the same symptoms. Sometimes another physical disease can cause depression; sometimes certain drugs used in combination produce symptoms of depression. Steroids can account for the mood swings of depression, and long-term use of alcohol and street drugs can worsen the symptoms.

Medication is useful in treating depression because it works on the source of the problem in the brain. Without going into detail, suffice it to say that whatever goes wrong in the firing of neurotransmitters in the brain, specific medication can work to correct the problem.

The typical antidepressants used are the MAOs (mentioned in the section on Anxiety) or the tricyclics, which are safer to use (since MAOs require a restricted diet) but may take up to eight weeks to work.

Prozac has recently been found to be effective in reducing the symptoms of depression without the concomitant problem of weight gain. Unfortunately, it has a side effect in a very small percentage of cases: aggressive and violent behavior.

MANIC DEPRESSION

Everyone has highs and lows, but for the person suffering from manic depression (or bipolar disorder) the highs and lows are out of control. The highs are marked by excessive energy, poor judgment, inability to sleep, and sometimes combativeness and delusions. The lows are marked by periods of preoccupation with suicide.

Evelyn introduced me to manic depression back in 1973. She was admitted in a manic state to the state hospital where I worked. She was brought to the ward and almost immediately dragged to the seclusion room, swinging her fists and cursing at the top of her lungs. Her long, whitish hair lay tangled on her shoulders; her face was painted thickly with makeup, and her clothes were in tatters from wrestling the male aides all the way over from admissions. Other than that, Evelyn looked like anyone's sixty-three-year-old grandmother.

When someone is "on a high" like that, he or she has no control over his impulses. He may spend money he doesn't have (writing bad checks), buy things he doesn't need, or invest in schemes he would normally avoid. You cannot reason with him. All you can do is see that he gets treatment, and the most humane forms are medication and a secure environment. These people will not accept your advice to see a doctor; often this person ends up in a hospital against his or her will. They actually *LIKE* the feeling of mania and loss of control, although everyone around them does *not*.

Lithium is the drug of choice in manic depression. Actually it is a salt, not a drug, and it works to restore the balance in mood. It brings the manic person down while preventing a descent to suicide. When it works, it is very effective. But Lithium must reach therapeutic levels in the bloodstream. If it exceeds those levels, it can induce vomiting and other unpleasant, even deadly side effects. If it does not reach the correct level it is not effective. Again, the side effects must be weighed carefully against the benefits.

Some therapists have used major tranquilizers instead, especially if medical factors worked against the use of Lithium. The major tranquilizers such as Thorazine and Haldol have worked on the violent behavior and the perceptual disorder but did not always correct the mood. And for some people they are far more disagreeable to take.

SCHIZOPHRENIA

Schizophrenia does not mean "split personality." Dr. Jekyll did not turn into Mr. Hyde because he was suffering from this disease. Rather, schizophrenics suffer from disordered thinking and consequently an inability to function. Schizophrenics live in their own world, which may not even be familiar from one schizophrenic to the next. They usually exhibit signs of confusion and disorientation. They often hear voices—commanding voices that emanate from the television set. These are called hallucinations because they are not real. Schizophrenics often experience "ideas of reference"; they believe that everything that happens around them somehow centers on them. They may also suffer from delusions, usually paranoid ideas such as someone's wanting to do them harm. The schizophrenic is so wrapped up in his bizarre thinking that he has lost the capacity to function in the world. For that reason almost all schizophrenics require treatment at some point.

If the word schizophrenic makes you think first of John Hinckley, who shot President Ronald Reagan in 1981, you probably think that all schizophrenics are dangerous. Of course, some are dangerous because they listen to voices that have nothing to do with reality. Once Dwain worked with a man diagnosed as paranoid schizophrenic who had been ordered by his voices to shoot Dwain. Immediate hospitalization and medication managed the man's impulse and muted the voices that controlled his life and threatened to end Dwain's.

But not all schizophrenics are violent. I once "case-managed" three women who lived together in an apartment. They had spent over half of their lives in a state hospital but now had been released to manage on their own. I used to take them shopping or to the park once a week, and I would check to see if they were taking their medication or having any problems. I was supposedly helping to resocialize them.

One afternoon I arrived to find Beryl waiting for me on the front stairs. We planned to go to a fancy department store, so she was all spruced up in her best dress, hat, and high heels. But the startling feature was her knee-high nylon stockings that were never meant to be worn with a short dress. I politely suggested that she might change to longer stockings, but she would have none of it; she was ready to go. On many other occasions I had to suggest better ways for them to dress. Being so many years alone in their own little world had made them all but incapable of deciding how to fit in with our world.

Another difference with these women was that they were totally humorless. They never told a joke, and their expressions were just as flat and lifeless when I broke an appointment as when I announced the birth of one of my children.

If someone in your family has this disorder, you are probably well aware of the crimp it has put on your life-style. Schizophrenics may suffer from sleep disturbance and wander around at night. They may act impulsively and in inappropriate ways. They can be counted on to say the wrong thing at the wrong time.

The schizophrenic does not always know the appropriate places to express sexual urges. Some masturbate in public; others fall prey to people bent on sexually abusing them.

Schizophrenia is one of the most disturbing disorders for two reasons. First, it is embarrassing (not to mention scary) to see those you love acting inappropriately. Second, the disorder is difficult to treat and to date cannot be cured. Major tranquilizers have been effective in reducing the symptoms, so that nowadays schizophrenics don't have to live their lives in mental institutions. On the other hand the major tranquilizers have miserable side effects. Haldol is frequently implicated in dystonic reactions, the drawing up of facial and neck muscles. Thorazine increases sun sensitivity, so that one can end up with severe burns or even sunstroke. Mellaril, which supposedly has the least side effects, can cause temporary impotence. The worst side effect of all is irreversible. Called tardive dyskinesia, it is the result of too much major tranquilizer over too long a period of time. A person with tardive dyskinesia makes involuntary repetitious movements of the fingers and mouth, as if he were rolling a pill around in his fingers or trying to lick a crumb back into his mouth. He may grimace uncontrollably. Doctors have become more sensitive to this development and carefully monitor dosages.

Lesser side effects of the major tranquilizers are blurred vision, dry mouth, and occasional light-headedness. Doctors keep track of the degree of discomfort from the side effects in order to reduce or alter the medication to best suit the person. Schizophrenia does not mean the end of the world that it once meant; however, according to *Mental Illness: A Home Care Guide* by Dr. Aristide Esser and Sylvia Lacey, "25 percent will recover and 50 percent will lead fulfilling lives at home." Not comforting statistics for those who fall in the other 25 percent.

DEMENTIA

On a trip back home to Maine many years ago, I learned that a favorite former teacher had developed Alzheimer's disease. I was torn between the desire to see Mr. Johns and the fear that he would be embarrassed to have me witness his condition. In the end, I called his wife to ask about him. Mrs. Johns said that he would not recognize me anymore, even though ten years earlier he had treated me like a daughter. He was halfway through the course of the disease and was already getting lost just walking down the front steps. He wandered around the house at night, not recognizing his wife who tried to keep him from hurting himself. My heart sank. I knew the prognosis of Alzheimer's: victims get worse until eventually they become combative with family members who they fear are trying to harm them. They can't eat or sleep and more than likely succumb to physical problems that can no longer be managed.

Mr. Johns had been a dynamic teacher who believed in teaching children by setting a strong positive example. I had admired his strength and his convictions even if I had not always agreed with them. This was not the man I wanted to remember. I chose not to see him, and he died three years ago while his wife was making plans to place him in a nursing home. But had he been my father instead of an old and treasured teacher, how could I not have seen him—slowly dying every day? And how much more it would have hurt me to see my father a virtual child again.

Dementia, of which Alzheimer's is only one disease, is another name for senility. It is a disease of the brain that cannot be altered with medication. Some symptoms—for example, combativeness and aggression—can be managed with medicines, but otherwise the progression of the disease cannot be stopped. Brain cells do not regenerate, and as the disease progresses more cells are damaged, affecting the person's memory and ability to take care of himself. His personality gradually changes, and he may become aggressive out of frustration with his limited abilities and anger with an environment he increasingly finds confusing. He may have crying spells because of his frailties or perhaps in more lucid moments when he realizes what is happening to him. As the disease progresses, he may behave more and more inappropriately and be unable to listen to reason. He will not accept that he cannot drive a car anymore, and he won't listen to advice about what to wear. He does not know where to go to the bathroom, and if you intervene he may hit you. Most hurtful of all, he may end up not knowing you. Medicine cannot change this behavior; it can only help manage him or her.

Nothing can be done to reverse the course of dementia, but you can examine how you respond to the person who has it. Perhaps the greatest gift you can offer the afflicted person is acceptance.

PTSD

PTSD, which stands for post traumatic stress disorder, has become more commonly recognized now that the Vietnam veterans have brought it to light. It does not refer only to people who have survived war trauma; it applies equally to women who have endured years of physical and sexual abuse or children who have been terrorized by gunmen in their playground. According to *Mental Illness: A Home Care Guide,* PTSD "appears after a psychologically traumatic event that is outside the usual range of human experiences."

People with PTSD appear guarded, trying to avoid

anything that might evoke a memory or feeling they might not be able to control. If provoked, they can become vigilant and focused as if looking for that which they want to forget.

Dwain has worked with many Vietnam veterans. A recurring theme with them is their attempt to distinguish reality, or put more simply, to keep the past from intruding on the present. They can drive through town thinking all the while that Vietcong will pop out any minute from behind parked cars. Some men tell of hearing a car backfire and—thinking it is a sniper—throwing themselves down on the sidewalk and covering their head. One of Dwain's clients said he spotted people gathering on rooftops and ducked for cover from the snipers. He later learned they were watching a ship coming into port.

As you can imagine, a person suffering from PTSD lives a tortured existence, always on guard against perceived threats, always afraid of evoking his own memories of the trauma. Certain smells can trigger memories; sounds—particularly helicopters or planes flying overhead—can bring back the dreaded memory.

Supportive counseling, long-term psychotherapy (more on that later), and periodic hospitalization in severe cases can help the person in his struggle to fit back into society. Medication may be prescribed to treat the symptoms of anxiety or depression or sleeplessness. In earlier times Thorazine and Mellaril were given to dampen the aggressive impulses, but they were probably given more to appease family members than to help the sufferer himself. Misunderstanding PTSD, people thought everyone afflicted with it was either psychotic or about to be. Psychotropic drugs (major tranquilizers) can be given when the person is agitated, but they cannot be relied on to induce a major transformation.

CHAPTER ◇ 2

How Much Can You Help?

When someone is said to have an emotional problem, realize that the problem does not start and end with that person. Linda Davis was an attractive young teenager whom I treated. She appeared to be a bubbly, outgoing cheerleader all set to finish her last year of high school when she came to my office. She had tried to hang herself the night before. She was alive only because her parents had come home early from a party and surprised her in the garage.

To say merely that Linda was depressed would be an insult to your intelligence. She was, of course, depressed. However, Linda was very good at pretending to be happy and "normal" because that was what she thought people (especially her parents) wanted to see. Linda was far from happy. In our first session she told me that she thought she had an eating problem because she perceived herself as too fat and her parents were always trying to make her eat. She dieted constantly, and then gorged when no one was home. Her family had recently moved from another town, and although she was popular, she felt alone and empty.

When I met with her family, I found yuppie-looking parents and a plainer older sister. Everyone seemed to want to view the "problem" as Linda's, although they all had some degree of anxiety about living with a suicidal person. Mrs. Davis said she was afraid to leave Linda alone for fear she might try to hurt herself again—and she didn't want to come home and find Linda's lifeless body in the living room. Mr. Davis said he couldn't figure out what Linda had to be depressed about because she was so pretty and had so much to look forward to. (Adults are always saying that sort of thing, as if they have forgotten all the hassles they experienced growing up.) He worried about her dieting because he thought she'd wind up like those skinny kids who stopped eating and had to be tube-fed. So he was always telling her to eat something. Naturally, the more Linda's parents treated her as the vulnerable little girl they saw, the more she retreated into silence and anger.

Linda's sister, Marge, was a study in suppressed rage. She viewed Linda as the spoiled baby sister who got from their parents more than she ever got. She fumed through most of the meeting because she had had to come down from college to attend it, and she clearly didn't think her sister worth the time or energy. Marge did not want to have to be responsible for her sister's well-being, and as a matter of fact simply wanted to be left out.

So where do family members fit into the life of the patient or client? Do they go overboard and orchestrate the person's life as if he or she were not capable of making any decision at all? Or do they withdraw because they don't want to be bothered by problems they don't understand? In this chapter we shall look at the needs of the person with an emotional disorder and see how you—the teenager—can adjust to life with him or her.

Obviously, it makes a difference how the person is related to you. If it is your mother or father, it is certainly much harder to avoid the whole issue of something being wrong. If it is an aunt, an uncle, or a grandparent, sometimes you can get away with sticking your head in the sand and pretending everything is normal. If the person is a sibling, it may depend on your closeness in age (or temperament); the closer you are to him or her, the harder his or her problems will hit you.

Some of you may be like Marge Davis, wanting nothing to do with "the problem." Unfortunately, not wanting to get involved doesn't mean that you can go on living in the same house—or visiting the same people—without facing up to certain realities. You cannot assume that others will deal with the problems (or relatives), so you don't have to. It is not helpful—certainly not conducive to recovery—to pretend that things in your family are "normal" when they are not. If families are secretive about certain members, they are saying in effect that there is something shameful about these people.

People who are emotionally ill have the same needs that we all do—to be loved for what they are and treated with respect. They do not cause their illness in most cases, and they don't cease being members of your family because their ability to function has changed. Turning your back on these people says that you are ashamed of them (and perhaps their relationship to you) or that you feel incapable of giving them loving support. Neither of those has to be true.

Let's say you are living with someone who has been diagnosed as having schizophrenia or some other form of disorganized thinking and confusion. A person whose inner world is already stretched to the limit by overstimulation needs a calmer structured environment. You can help by not bringing half of your math class home for lunch or holding that pajama party in the room next to your relative's. Obviously, you must make concessions so that your relative can remain at home. Of course, it doesn't mean that you must lead a cloistered life either. You can bring home one or two sensitive friends who know that you are living with someone recovering from an emotional disorder. Your relative needs as little additional stress as possible, so limiting the number of visitors is important.

You might find yourself in the role of confidante. As a teenager, that is an inappropriate role for you. You may want to take part in family therapy sessions to understand your role in "the problem," but you should in no way appoint yourself "case manager" for your relative. You do not dole out medication and monitor his or her taking it properly. You can lend a sympathetic ear as a friend, but you do not put yourself in the position of amateur therapist because it will backfire on you. Therapists never treat their own family members. Therapy is better left to professionals, who are paid to be objective.

You might find yourself assuming more than a teenager's share of household chores if it is your mother or father who is incapacitated by illness. As long as you are not helping to pretend that nothing is wrong by covering for him or her, it is a way to make yourself useful and to show that you care.

I once got involved in a community project in which I assisted some store owners in dealing with chronically mentally ill customers. They asked me how they should treat these people, some of whom were schizophrenics and "talked to themselves" in public.

"What should we do when they walk out without paying their bill?" they asked me.

"What would you do if someone else walked out without paying?" I asked.

"We'd either yell at him or call the police," they said.

"Well, what's the problem?"

"Well, we didn't want to do that to *them.*"

"Why not?" I asked.

"Because, well, they're not, you know, they're not right in the head."

"What do you think would happen?" I asked.

"They might *really* go crazy," they said, as if pleading with me to understand what they were talking about.

"First of all," I said, "you have to remember that these people are still people, usually capable of understanding right from wrong. If they behave inappropriately and you ask them to stop, and they don't, you have a right to call the police. They, in turn, have the right to be treated just like the rest of us who are not allowed to sneak out without paying."

"Well, how about if we called the hospital?" the store owners invariably asked me. "Couldn't you guys just come out and get him?"

"No," I said. "We don't do that."

"Why not?"

"Because the person has a right to be treated as an ordinary citizen. You don't haul ordinary citizens off to an institution simply because *you* think they're crazy. You can't lock someone up because he acts weird or you're afraid of him."

Of course, I didn't leave it at that. Obviously, the townspeople saw our former patients as threatening, and it was to everyone's benefit to help them all get along. Sometimes I encouraged the store owners to tolerate the idiosyncrasies of the ex-patients. After all, I had seen ordinary citizens around town who looked a lot stranger. At other times I encouraged the store owners to be more specific with their customers about what behavior was allowed and what wasn't. I also encouraged them to establish some kind of relationship with these people, because mutual acceptance increased in direct proportion to the level of understanding.

All these ideas can be applied in your own family. If you live with someone who has been chronically mentally ill, he or she may often need to be reminded *how to act in public*. Being direct (without showing shame or disgust) about what he needs to wear or how he should behave is something you can easily do. You don't have to treat the person like a baby; you merely have to accept that *right now* he is not capable of using good judgment and can benefit from yours.

As hard as it may be, *don't judge these people*. You may have to reassess your expectations of them, particularly with brain-damaged persons, but you do not fault them for being less than you would like. Not judging them means not expecting speedy recovery from their illness and not holding them responsible for changing *your* life. Humor goes a long way in helping both of you survive this period—compassionate humor, not jokes at their expense.

What should you do if your relative becomes violent or threatens to hurt himself? First of all, you never jump between the person and a weapon. You would be surprised how strong irrational people can be when they have their mind set on doing something. Even your mother or father could be too confused to recognize you and would think you were intervening to hurt him or her. If the person does not appear dangerous but is merely rude or inappropriate, you might firmly request the appropriate behavior. Remember, however, that your relative may be offended by a "youngster" giving orders. You may have to defer to other adults.

If you are concerned about your relative's well-being while he or she lives with you, you should be involved in the treatment planning. If you have not been asked, you can request to meet with other family members, the patient, and the therapist to discuss care and treatment goals so that if problems arise you would know what to do or whom to call for assistance.

If you are afraid that your relative may try to kill himself, you should be involved in case management meetings or family therapy sessions. The therapist is trained to monitor the client's state of mind, but you can point out to him or her things you've observed that alarm you.

Dwain once gave a lecture to some Emergency Medical Technicians, who wanted to know how to tell when someone would actually take his own life. Dwain could not help them because no one knows how to tell if someone will go through with a suicide plan. You can only make an educated guess based on the person's circumstances, the likelihood that things will improve for him in the near future, how seriously the person wants to die, how distorted his thinking is, and whether he has the means to carry out his plan—such as a bottle of pills or a gun. Obviously, if things have reached that point, the person needs to be in a hospital, where he can be under constant supervision. That watchfulness is not a job for you, the teenager.

Returning to what you can do if your relative is threatening you or himself, first keep yourself (and others) out of harm's way. If you have time and the situation does not appear life-threatening, call the person's therapist. If it is life-threatening, bear in mind that the person can be too confused to recognize you or know what he is doing. Get away and call the police; they are trained to handle these situations and equipped to transport the person to the hospital.

Recently a daughter of one of Dwain's clients called Dwain to say that her father had locked himself in his bedroom and was threatening to kill himself. Dwain stayed on the phone with the teenager, who called through the door to her father to make sure he was still alive. Dwain heard her pleading with him to unlock the door and at least talk with Dwain, but he refused to do either. Finally Dwain told her to say that he was calling the police to come and take her father to a hospital. Angry at the intrusion, the client unlocked the door and came out, but the daughter was beside herself at feeling as if she had held her father's life in her hands.

You face an added problem when your relative does not believe he or she is ill or acting out of the ordinary. If your relative—let's say it is your mother—seems unduly depressed and unable to get through the day, you might sit down with her, tell her that she doesn't seem herself anymore, and admit that you are worried about her. Don't be surprised if she rejects your view: "Oh, I'm just having a bad day; everything's really okay." Persist, because deep down your mother will know that she is not feeling "right."

You might suggest that she see someone at a community mental health center to evaluate her problem; or if that sounds too threatening to her (as if you're accusing her of being "crazy"), suggest that she see the family physician.

You may not be able to get through to your loved one, or she may be too disturbed to have any insight into her condition. In such case you will have to enlist the support of others in reaching her. Talk to another adult—a teacher at school, your family doctor, or make the call yourself to a mental health center. They can suggest ways of encouraging your relative to come in and be evaluated. However, in the event your mother (or whoever) is "out of control," don't try to bargain to get her to a hospital. Simply call the police, or if others seem to have the situation under control, *stay out of the way*. Wrestling with an unmanageable person (especially your own mother) will look demeaning, but it is important that she get to a safe environment and get the help she needs.

There are many people you can turn to for help with your relative; the merits of each are discussed in Chapter 5: your minister, your family physician, and the case manager or therapist in charge of your relative's case. You should have access to each of their telephone numbers in case of emergency—or sometimes just for your own support. Living with emotional stress is draining for everyone in the vicinity.

CHAPTER ◇ 3

Maintaining a Relationship During and Afterward

Several years ago I broke the ring finger on my left hand. I didn't think to take my wedding band off immediately, and by the time I got to the doctor's office my finger was too swollen to get the ring off. Well, I wasn't about to have the doctor cut that beautiful band off, so to avoid that I promised to follow to the letter everything he said.

"Well, if you keep it packed in ice and don't use it for a while, you might be lucky," he said. "Otherwise, I'm going to have to cut the ring off."

For that whole evening our kids were very helpful and considerate of my immobilized hand. By the next morning, though, their patience was wearing thin, and Dwain was not around to demand better behavior of them.

Our oldest child, then six, said, "Can we do a craft project today, Mom?"

"I'm sorry, Michal," I said, "but the doctor doesn't want me to use this hand. I'm supposed to keep it still."

Michal looked at me with obvious disgust. "How are things supposed to get done around here?" she asked.

"Well, I guess the doctor thought my kids would help me out," I said.

"Oh, come on," she said. "Didn't you tell the doctor how *old* we are?"

Later in the day my three-year-old, carrying an armload of stuffed animals, approached me. One tumbled out of her arms onto the floor in front of me.

"Could you pick that up for me, Mommy?" she said.

"How about if *you* pick it up?" I said. "Mommy has a broken finger, remember?"

"Just use your *other* hand, Mommy," Jaime said.

After only one day of sympathy, the kids were telling me they had had their fill of "doing" for me. If they had been able to put their feelings into words, they might have owned up to resentment at my continued disability or anger that I was such a weight around their little necks.

In this chapter, we shall look at some of the ways you might feel about a loved one's being ill. Mentally ill, that is, which is less accepted by society and not always easy to cure. Remember, when you are involved with someone having an emotional disorder, you are not likely to be surrounded by understanding people.

First, bear in mind that the strength of your emotional response will depend on how close you are to the relative, how serious the disorder is, and the potential for recovery.

Remember, too, that this chapter is in no way a blueprint for all the feelings in the world. You won't necessarily feel all these things or even any of these things; people vary in their capacity to handle stress. But if you do feel any of these emotions, you need not hate yourself for not being the perfect son or daughter. What is important is to recognize the feeling and do something constructive with it. Pretending that you don't have bad feelings about your loved one will only make your suffering worse. Whether you admit them or not, the feelings are still there.

Andy, a nice kid in eleventh grade, came from a family that set high standards for achievement. Of the three children, Andy—the middle child—seemed likeliest to make the grade. He worked hard, he got excellent grades, and he was a basketball star. There wasn't much he couldn't do.

Except get some attention at home.

Andy had an older brother, Henry, who had been diagnosed with a variety of things by the time he was a teenager. Henry was accused of having an attentional problem, of being oppositional, and sometimes of being antisocial (although that diagnosis is formally reserved for people over eighteen). Since no one really knew what was "wrong" with Henry, his parents spent a lot of time and money running from agency to agency and doctor to doctor trying to find someone who could make him fall in line. In the meantime, "Horrible Henry" (as Andy secretly called him) remained the focus of the entire family. A younger sister withdrew, nurturing an artistic talent, but Andy kept garnering achievement awards, though no one at home noticed. The more Andy thought about his brother, the madder he got. Even when his father took him aside and tried to explain Henry's problems, Andy was unmoved.

"I should be relieved it's him and not me that has the problems," he said. "But mostly what I feel is plain old jealousy. I mean, I'm the 'good son', aren't I? I'm not the one disrupting all the classes, getting in trouble with the cops every Friday night. But who do my parents spend their every waking minute worrying about? Him. Horrible Henry."

Sometimes jealousy leads to even stronger feelings of resentment. The "sick" person is getting all the attention, taking up the family time and energy, or else ruining the quality of life for others in the household. Don't be surprised if you suddenly find yourself wishing the person were dead.

He won't really die simply because you wish it so. When you're that angry, though, it is wise to find an appropriate outlet for your feelings. Sometimes you can feel better just by acknowledging how you feel to another adult or an understanding peer, or by writing in a journal. Writing can have a purging effect on bottled-up feelings, and later when you look back on those times you can gauge how far you've come (or sunk) since then.

Don't let people shame you for feeling angry. It is a logical (if misunderstood) emotion, and you're not a bad person for feeling it.

Sometimes it is useful to dig beneath the anger and see what more is hiding there. After Dwain and I lost our second child (he died at birth), I was so angry I couldn't see straight. That anger got me through weeks when I might otherwise have given up. That anger kept me alive. When I stopped to look past the anger, I found intense longing and wrenching grief, emotions too overwhelming for me to have handled in the beginning. But by focusing on the anger I had kept from feeling my biggest hurt—the overwhelming sense of loss.

When we are angry at loved ones for being ill, it often goes back to our loss. These people (especially parents, who according to an unwritten law are always supposed to be there for us) let us down when they became sick. Even though on one level we might know they did not purposely choose to suffer this way, it does not change the fact that they *are* ill and *are not the way they used to be.* The sadness over the loss of the "normal" person is what sparks our anger, but, unfortunately, the anger is what we feel.

One last word about anger: It does not readily go away, even when you recognize it. That may be because it reflects our own helplessness to "fix" the loved one who is ill. Whatever the reason, sometimes it helps to have a physical release for all that emotion. Taking up a sport that saps your energy or doing some hard physical chores will help get rid of some of that emotion.

I once worked with a woman who made remarkable progress in a period of weeks, going from being actively suicidal on admission to the hospital to a stronger, angry woman who did not see self-destruction as the only way out. Even after discharge from the hospital, however, she was still depressed. A few weeks after she had been released, her daughters called me at home.

"Mom isn't better yet," they said. "You've got to take her back. She's still not her old self."

"What's wrong?" I asked, knowing that we could never keep people in a hospital long enough to restore them completely.

"Well, she still has crying spells," they said.

"Yes, she probably will have those for a while. That's why she is in outpatient therapy. Is she suicidal?"

"She hasn't said anything about killing herself," one of her daughters said.

"And is she eating and sleeping?" I asked.

"Not as much as we'd like," they said.

"Are you worried about her in general?" I asked.

"I guess we just think she should be well by now. It's been over two months now, you know."

"Yes, I know," I said, "but unfortunately, there is no timetable for recovery. Impatience with your mother's progress won't make her get better faster; it will just make her feel more of a failure."

You might find yourself feeling embarrassed as much as angry or impatient, especially if you don't understand emotional disorders. Depression, anxiety, and thought disorders are real illnesses, just as much as diabetes and broken legs. The only difference is that physical ailments are more acceptable to society. Broken legs are visible, whereas psychic wounds are not. Some people do not believe in what they can't see.

And society can be so damning.

When I was in fifth grade, the mother of one of my classmates hanged herself from the rafters in the barn. Candace and her siblings had not known that day when they got off the school bus that their mother was dead in the barn.

Mrs. Mathews had been depressed ever since her father (Candace's grandfather) had died several months earlier. When she left the note, "Gone with Father" on the dining room table, the kids assumed she meant that she had gone into town with *their* father. When their father returned without her, the family understood which father she had joined and, looking in the barn, discovered her body.

I can't describe how awful I felt when my mother told me about Mrs. Mathews. Maybe I was a little ashamed at being relieved that it was Candace's mother, not mine. In those days nobody talked much about suicide—and *never* about depression, which most people thought was the weak person's way of giving in to life's problems. Nobody talked to our class about Candace—what we should say, how we should act. The first day she came back to school we were all afraid of her. Mostly we didn't want to say the wrong thing, not knowing there was a "right" thing to say. As horrible as it is to admit now, some of us were disgusted by her, as if her mother's "disease" (her depression) was dirty or catching. We were afraid something might be "wrong" with Candace too, something we might catch if we hung around with her. So a little bunch of ten-year-olds further isolated and condemned a lonely, grieving little girl. I am still disgusted—with myself.

If your relative has a type of disorder that makes him behave inappropriately or say rude things, you will naturally be afraid to take him or her out in public. If he or she offends someone it will reflect badly on you. Someone who has been taking psychotropic medications and has signs of tardive dyskinesia may act so strangely that you are afraid for others to see him or her and associate the two of you.

Yes, people will stare at your relative, and yes, you may hear frightened children ask what is wrong with him or her. We live in a curious—no, make that *nosy*—society, and you cannot isolate your loved one simply because you fear others will make *you* feel uncomfortable. Ignore what you can, anticipate (and avoid) crowds when you can, and demonstrate acceptance yourself. It is easier for others to show embarrassment or disgust if you show it first.

Some people get discouraged over their relative's illness, either wondering how much of the problem they have been or why they have to watch the person's decline. Remember that a disorder of this magnitude did not arise because you were not a model child. Your behavior cannot "make" someone start hallucinating or become suicidal. We are not that powerful, no matter what we think.

Dwain talked to a girl in the emergency room of a hospital shortly after she had slashed both her wrists. Anne was an emotional mess, especially when she saw Dwain; she associated him with the place where her "crazy" father went once a week for therapy. Even though her symptoms were different from her father's (who was a schizophrenic), she feared she would turn out to be just like him because it was "all in the family."

It is true that some disorders do run in families, and doctors are not certain why. Worrying will not improve your odds, but familiarizing yourself with the disorder will help you spot warning signs should any develop.

Lastly, you might be frightened—frightened of things you don't understand and, more significantly, of your loved one's dying.

The more you understand, the less mysterious the disorder becomes. The more you surround yourself with people who are in the same boat, the more support you'll have. Get acquainted with those who take care of your relative—the therapists, doctors, or case managers. Read up on the disorder, and have your questions answered by those familiar with your relative. Become involved with a support group for families of the mentally ill such as the state and local Alliance for the Mentally Ill and the Siblings and Adult Children Network. Sometimes mental health centers offer groups or workshops on living with the chronically ill. Join them, as much for the friendships they offer as for the information.

Simply understanding your relative's condition and surrounding yourself with others who are in the same boat are not enough, however. You may still be angry that life has handed you this problem. Recognizing your anger and finding an outlet for it are only the beginning. For your peace of mind, you have to face certain realities. Your relative may be emotionally unstable for the rest of his or her life. You may feel like the parent yourself at times. The reality is unfortunate, unfair, but nevertheless *the way things are.*

But that does not mean that you have to resign yourself to your loss. We all need to be nurtured and cherished, and if your parent is unable to show you this constancy of love, you might find it with somebody else. Surely an aunt, an uncle, even a teacher can cherish you enough to compensate to some extent for that primary loss.

For example, not all abused children grow up to be abusers themselves. How do these young adults keep from repeating their parents' mistakes? More than likely, they found an adult whom they could trust and used that person as a substitute role model. What they might not have gotten at home, they found in someone else. Some call these people mentors.

You are still a good person and deserving of love even if your emotionally unstable parent cannot show it all the time. Accept your parent's limitations, do something constructive with your anger, and allow another relative to nurture you along the way.

Grief over the impending loss of a relative (for example, one with Alzheimer's) is similar to any loss, but it will be a continual loss until the actual death takes place. To keep the feelings from overwhelming you, you must find acceptable ways of letting the feelings out. Recognize the impending loss; do or say what you must so that you have no regrets about your last days, weeks, or months with your loved one; do something good for yourself each day, even if it's only taking a twenty-minute bubble bath; share your grief with a friend. Above all else, keep the faith. If that means praying for recovery or a painless end, pray. If it means meditating for peace, do that instead.

A relative's baby was born with a failing liver. Surgery offered a 50 percent chance of living. Without surgery, he would die. The family opted for the surgery and started to pray. They hoped; they prayed; they were not going to let that baby die. No one else held out much hope.

Remarkably, the baby survived and is now a healthy five-year-old.

It doesn't hurt to hope.

Let's assume that someone in your family has been hospitalized for an emotional disorder. How will that affect you? More than likely, you will be asked to participate in family meetings along with the patient. That is so the doctor and therapist (whether a social worker, psychologist, or psychiatric nurse) can find out more about the circumstances at home leading up to the illness. It is not done so that the therapist can assign blame to any one of you. People don't live in a vacuum, and problems don't suddenly arise without anyone's being aware of them. The therapist simply needs to get as many different perspectives as possible. Use these family meetings to answer your own questions about what is happening. The more talking done in the open, the less chance that the family will close itself up in shame. Visit with your relative, and remind him or her that he is still loved. Don't just assume that he will know that if you show up every Sunday afternoon to see him. Make sure he hears you say the words. Let him know that you are not ashamed or disappointed in him (and if you *are*, you can bet he'll sense it, so find some appropriate way to work those feelings out).

Once your loved one is back at home, be sure you know the treatment plan for recovery, because you don't want to sabotage it. How could you possibly sabotage it? If you did not realize the importance of a manic depressive's staying on his medicine, for instance, you might encourage him to stop taking it now that he's better. Going off medication prematurely can lead to relapse. Don't play doctor with your relative; if you think you know what should be done for him, talk to the therapist first.

How you adjust to having the emotionally unstable person at home depends on how you handle your feelings and can meet your relative's needs. (Remember, you're not meant to meet all his needs.) Understanding what he is going through—and what you yourself are feeling—will make the adjustment easier. Most family members with a chronically ill relative say that their major complaint is not being part of the treatment. Don't become a part of that condemning society that says emotional problems should be kept in the dark. Your loved one is still a human being. Hang in there and support him or her, and above all, *accept him as he is*.

PART ◇ II

WHEN IT HAPPENS TO YOU

CHAPTER ◇ 4

How Do You Know What Is Wrong?

You probably know that adolescence is a time when no one quite feels normal, so sometimes what constitutes an emotional problem can be downright mystifying. Most teenagers have been through times when they felt depressed or "stressed out" or thought the end of the world was right around the corner.

And they were normal. . .

Adolescent emotions are heightened by the rush of hormones through the body, the discovery of all those new sexual feelings, and the awkwardness of a body growing faster than the spirit. Teenagers take each day more seriously than adults, who have usually experienced enough to realize that all things pass in time. So how do you know when something *is* wrong?

Mostly, it is a matter of *persistence* and *degree* of symptoms. If a depression lasts longer than a few days or weeks, or your symptoms interfere with your doing schoolwork or getting through the day, it is time to do something about it. Simply put, you need outside help to restore equilibrium to your life, to put things back in order.

Most teenagers tell me they feel a little crazy at times; most adults tell me teenagers *are* a little crazy at times.

So before you think you have a bona fide emotional disorder, consider first that you might be a normal teenager during abnormal times. Or perhaps it is bizarre circumstances in your life that are making you feel as if you're crazy. For example, victims of child abuse typically grow up thinking something is wrong with them because they can't adjust to their family life. The abused preadolescent typically accepts his life as being like everyone else's. It is not until he is a teenager that he realizes, "Hey, everyone else *doesn't* live like this!"

If you find yourself in a "crazy" environment where you have been verbally, sexually, or physically abused—or even threatened—understand that you are not crazy; it is the circumstances, the surroundings.

I once treated a woman who had been sexually abused by her older brother for years. Beth was now thirty-three years old and described herself as both empty and full of anger. As a child she had often been left in her brother's care. Beth, who had never felt much love from her parents, was starved for affection, so when her brother started making advances to her she interpreted them as expressions of love. On the one hand, she liked his petting her and giving her special treats for cooperating; on the other hand, she somehow felt that what he was doing was wrong. The abuse, which eventually included intercourse, continued until her brother moved away from home. In all that time Beth had never been able to tell her parents; she left them clues—blood on the bedsheets, hickeys on her neck—but no one asked her about them. By the time her brother left, Beth was a withdrawn, fearful young woman. She had closed down all emotions, mostly, she said, so she wouldn't have to feel that overwhelming rage about his robbing her of her childhood.

Beth was not "crazy"; she was abused.

Tara was another girl who grew up in a "crazy" household. In hers, the abuse was not overt; the household was simply chaotic. Her parents were engaged in an open marriage; each partner not only felt free to sleep with anyone but to bring that person into the home. Tara said that on many mornings she didn't know which parent was in which bedroom and with whom.

The problems increased when another couple moved in with Tara's family, and the adults played Let's Swap Spouses. The other man apparently grew tired of the games, and on one particularly crazy afternoon he shot himself in the living room. When Tara and her brother came home from school they found the body.

Tara's mother divorced her husband and moved out. Without her kids. Tara and Brandon were left with their father and their new stepmother of sorts.

In a household rampant with alcoholism and where the rules of propriety were constantly changing, it is small wonder Tara thought herself "crazy." She, too, was not, although she *was* traumatized by her circumstances.

Another woman I treated came from similar circumstances. Laurel was her mother's second illegitimate child. Her mother had given the first child up for adoption. She kept Laurel, but because she was an alcoholic she could not adequately care for the child and put her in a foster home until the age of four. When her mother married, she took Laurel back and moved to Iowa where her parents lived. Laurel remembers those years as being constantly torn between her parents' wishes ("Don't tell Grandma about our drinking") and her grandparents' strict moral standards. When Laurel's parents went out drinking for the evening, they took her with them, leaving her in the car behind the bar. Laurel was no safer when she was taken into the homes where her parents went to drink. On more than one occasion she was sexually molested there.

When Laurel was eight she got a baby sister—and a new job. Not only was she expected to do most of the household chores, but now she had to baby-sit this new child. Many were the evenings when Laurel was the only one at home with the baby—especially if her parents ended up in jail for the night for public drunkenness.

Over the years, the drinking and partying got worse. Eventually Laurel left home and got married at the age of fifteen. She promptly had five children (one set of twins), which insured her having enough responsibilities to last a lifetime.

Laurel was not crazy, even though she was very confused (and depressed) because of her upbringing. Children are not meant to be brought up in bars or in cars outside of bars. Children are not supposed to grow up vigilant around adults who might in a drunken moment mistake them for a sexual partner. And children—*with no exception*—are not meant to be sexual partners for any adult.

Laurel wrote me recently about her childhood—or lack of one. She said, "I believe being raised in an alcoholic and indifferent environment, I did not learn how to love or have faith in me. I feel that alcohol and indifference (partly caused by alcohol) have robbed me of. . . my emotions. Please try to put into your book that a child of alcoholic parents suffers emotionally and physically the rest of her life."

Teenage admissions to psychiatric hospitals have risen by 450 percent in the past decade, according to a recent NBC broadcast. Are the kids being hospitalized because of underindulgent parents, or do they have serious problems? Let's look at some of the emotional disorders that wreak havoc in the growing-up years. (Refer back to Chapter 1 for more information on each disorder.)

CONDUCT DISORDERS

When someone is diagnosed as having a conduct disorder, you can usually assume that that person has been having difficulty getting along with others, doing his schoolwork, or staying out of legal trouble. Conduct-disordered kids are not the teacher's pets, and they probably are not the kids that therapists look forward to working with each day. Teenagers in this category tend to be aggressive and constantly at odds with society. They sometimes lie, steal, and defy anthority, and they show little remorse for their actions. In fact, I'm describing them only briefly because conduct-disordered kids don't see anything wrong with their behavior; it is always the other person at fault. The conduct-disordered teenagers are not likely even to read this chapter, because nothing is wrong with *them*.

The problem really arises when you try to label someone conduct-disordered. Many kids *appear* conduct-disordered (and if they were over eighteen they might be called borderline or antisocial), but in truth they may have physical problems that contribute to the loss of emotional control. Others may be diagnosed as having attention deficit disorder (ADD), which means that the person has a learning disability, a poor attention span (unless he is relating to objects instead of people), or some degree of hyperactivity, impulsivity, or both. These kids, too, will be disruptive in the classroom, and will no doubt have worn their parents out before they reached their teens.

With limit-setting (sometimes in a structured environment outside of the home) and clearly defined boundaries and rules, the conduct-disordered person can improve enough to fit into society.

Some kids, however, have no desire to fit into society. They would prefer for society to fit in better with them. These teens are the budding antisocial adults who have no regard for anyone else's needs. Since no medication can give a person a conscience, these people do not change with ordinary psychotherapeutic tools. Dr. Stanton Samenow in his book, *Before It's Too Late*, has an entire treatment agenda for these types. He writes: "The antisocial youngster can thoroughly confuse others and sometimes gain sympathy by emphasizing how good his intentions were. He expects that focusing on his good intentions will obscure or at least mitigate the harmfulness of whatever he did." Again he writes: "The antisocial youngster is capable of experiencing guilt. But instead he [has] the capacity common to criminals, simply to shut off conscience long enough to do whatever [is] expedient or exciting at the moment."

The thing to remember with a conduct-disordered person is that he *violates the rights of others* because he has no control over his impulses (possibly ADD), he is preoccupied with his own problems (possibly depression), or he has no regard for anyone else (Samenow's antisocial youngster).

ADJUSTMENT REACTIONS

Teenagers who are diagnosed in this category seldom show a long history of symptoms or the severe reactions of another disorder, say manic depression. The clinician (the therapist who makes the initial diagnosis) may not want to burden the person with a more serious diagnosis. He or she assumes that the teenager is suffering symptoms of depression or anxiety because of a recent event. A teenager who reacts to a divorce or a new marriage by holing up in his room or losing interest in his schoolwork may be diagnosed as suffering from an adjustment reaction. In clinical terms, it means that the clinician assumes the teen will pull out of his depression in a short period of time. The diagnosis is not that important, actually, except to certain insurance companies, which will not pay for hospitalization for an adolescent adjustment reaction.

Ronald was an adolescent I treated. Fifteen years old, he was admitted to the hospital because he was on the verge of going to jail. His teachers could not handle him; they called him a wise guy. Ronald was at the hospital on a voluntary order, although he did not consider himself volunteering for treatment. "My mother said I had to come here," he told me.

"What's going on that she thought you needed treatment?" I asked.

"I'm always in trouble," he said.

"Well, how is that a problem?" I asked.

"I don't think anything *is* wrong with me if people would just stay off my back," he said.

Ronald could easily have been diagnosed as conduct-disordered because of his oppositional behavior. However, in family talks and in group therapy sessions Ronald showed how conflicted he was over his parents' divorce and, more significantly, his mother's dating again. Since his symptoms had not arisen until after the divorce, we considered that he was experiencing an adjustment reaction. We treated him as such, although he did respond to limit-setting and rules to manage his impulse to act out.

EATING DISORDERS

Among the hardest teens to work with are those with an eating disorder: anorexia (not eating) or bulimia (eating, but vomiting afterwards or using laxatives to purge the intestines). By the time a girl (I say "girl" because it is more often a female disorder) has been hospitalized, she is usually suffering physical signs of malnutrition, possible heart damage, and electrolyte imbalance (from dehydration). Her life is often hanging by a thread, and her weight has dropped below 100 pounds. The first order of business is to stabilize her *physical* condition. But the teenager by this point has lost all perspective and cannot make decisions for hereself. Usually, if she were consulted, she would strongly object to gaining weight. She sees no danger in her physical condition. She sees herself as fat, and no amount of reasoning can influence her. Some doctors believe that the teenager has a chemical imbalance in the brain that accounts for her perceptual distortions. Others suggest that advertising is to blame by touting the image of a skinny, sexy teenager as the epitome of acceptability.

Whatever the reason, the therapist has to work against that overwhelming desire not to eat. He or she has to get the person to eat, sometimes before he can help her understand why she has such a distorted self-image. Once medically stable, the teenager has the best chance for improvement if she enters a specialized program. She will need structure, possibly antidepressant medication, and group and individual therapy. It is a long, difficult process, not unlike that faced by long-term substance abusers.

Linda Davis (whom you may remember from Chapter 2) was developing an eating disorder when I knew her. She ate only when she thought no one was looking. She saw herself as fat and ugly, although in truth she was a gorgeous, lithe cheerleader. By the time I saw her (following her suicide attempt), she had no control over her eating. If she sat down to a meal, she would gobble up everything in sight. If she avoided food in the first place, she grew to *like* the gnawing feeling of hunger. Linda stopped treatment before I could help her make any meaningful changes. Admitting an eating disorder was too threatening to her at the time, and since I later moved out of state, I never learned if her symptoms worsened.

In the beginning stages of an eating disorder, you may find yourself cutting calories and increasing your level of exercise. As long as you are following a medically approved diet, nothing is wrong with that plan. Things go wrong, however, when the dieting becomes extreme, when whole meals are excluded from your diet. In time, as your body grows accustomed to starving (and it will slow its metabolism to fight starvation), you'll find you are drinking clear liquids (to avoid deadly calories) to fill the gnawing emptiness. You might alternate with bouts of eating everything in sight, only to vomit immediately before the calories have had time to be absorbed. By now you are unable to stop your self-destructive dieting, and ironically you can think of nothing but *food* all day long. You are controlled by that which you fear.

A woman I worked with in Maine was both anorexic and bulimic. Often such women have a history of sexual abuse, which was Kathy's case. Kathy had many admissions to Jackson Brook Institute in the two years I worked there. While she was not severely underweight, she was in danger of developing electrolyte problems, which can lead to heart attack and death. Kathy weighed about 100 pounds. She drank volumes of water in the belief that it would flush food out of her system and make her weigh less. She drank so much diet soda that we had to restrict her intake (which meant policing her, too, because she would not readily agree to any measure to help her gain weight).

Kathy understood that I wanted her to start eating regular meals, but that did not mean she agreed with me. She complied only when she was strictly supervised at mealtime and *after the meal*, so that she would not throw up what we had worked so hard to get into her. She got around eating so much by taking huge amounts of laxatives that she sneaked onto the ward. She would take fifty to sixty at a time even though she knew she was ravaging her digestive tract. It got to the point that every time she left the hospital grounds the nurses had to check her upon returning for the hidden stash of laxatives.

I can't claim that I helped to cure Kathy because when I last saw her she still had only minimal control over her need to abuse her body. I did come to understand her better and to like her.

You probably know that anorectics can and do die. If you are suffering from an eating disorder, you probably do not want to give up control over what you eat to a therapist. Without insight, you will not change your patterns of eating. And without getting physically healthier, you are not likely to develop insight or good judgment. It sounds like a vicious circle, and it is. The more unhealthy you become, the less likely you will be to "pull yourself out of it" on your own. You need psychological help.

COMPULSIONS

You read about obsessive-compulsive disorder in Chapter 1, but you may not have realized how common and how underreported it is. You remember that many people keep their rituals or repetitive thoughts hidden because they think others will consider them "crazy." OCD does not mean you are crazy, however; it means that something is out of kilter in your brain that makes you have to repeat certain behaviors or say certain things to keep tremendous anxiety at bay. In *The Boy Who Couldn't Stop Washing*, Dr. Judith Rapoport writes that 1 million adolescents in the U.S. have OCD and that male children with OCD outnumber females two to one.

If you even think you may have that disorder, I urge you to read Dr. Rapoport's book. People with OCD often started having symptoms—the repetitious thoughts, the rituals, the counting words or magic numbers over and over—when they were youngsters. They came to believe that this was how life was for everyone. Because of their preoccupations they have been misdiagnosed as schizophrenic. These kids, Dr. Rapoport has discovered, do not suffer from a perceptual disorder, but rather a biochemical change in the brain, which improves (and in many cases reverts to normal) with the administration of certain medications, particularly Anafranil.

SCHIZOPHRENIA

Childhood schizophrenia is a far more serious disorder because of the difficulty of treating it and the overall disruption of the afflicted person's life. As mentioned in Chapter 1, the schizophrenic is not a "split personality." He or she is not one person one minute and a completely different person the next. Instead, schizophrenia refers to the disorganization of the personality and the consequent inability to function. The person may hear voices that tell him to do something (kill himself or someone else, stay away from something, be afraid of someone who is out to harm him) and thus become immobilized: unable to make decisions or even to understand what other people want of him. He becomes unable to think straight in severe instances; he may be impulsive and inappropriate and suffer from sleep disturbances and an overall deadening of the emotions.

Remember, this is a range of possible symptoms. You need not develop them all to be diagnosed as schizophrenic. Furthermore, no diagnosis could be made without other information, including family background and a history of the symptoms.

Dakota was a young man I worked with who thought he was going crazy. Actually he was depressed, with the somewhat illogical thinking that goes with a severe and unrelenting depression. What made him think he was crazy, however, was that he had an older brother who literally was. Andrew was ten years older than Dakota and had suffered his first breakdown in college. He heard voices, stayed awake all hours of the night, and for weeks hung out in his room strumming a guitar. He couldn't relate to anyone about anything. Dakota thought that his symptoms attested to his own disorder. Because his brother was schizophrenic, he thought it was only a matter of time before he became so too.

Even though some conditions or vulnerabilities do run in families, that does not mean that you are destined to develop them.

Andrew had an entirely different disorder from Dakota's. Andrew's parents thought he had suffered a breakdown in college because he had smoked marijuana. I happened to know, however, that Andrew was having bizarre thoughts back in high school. He once gave me a birthday card; he had lovingly signed his name and then slashed across the card a Nazi swastika. Seeing this preoccupation with evil (as expressed in his frequent use of the swastika), I was frightened without knowing why. It was only later that I heard that Andrew had withdrawn into his own world of Nazis and bad guys and black thoughts. The marijuana probably only hastened his descent.

The prognosis for childhood schizophrenia is not encouraging—not if you have plans for a high-powered profession. Andrew has alternated between living in halfway houses (homes where people live semi-independently, supervised by an adult or health care worker) and being hospitalized. He is also dependent on medication (not addicted, though—there's a difference) to keep the voices from taking over his life.

Schizophrenics vary in their ability to function, but some people have been ill for so long that when they reach their late twenties they do not know how to behave in society. Many chronically ill people can benefit additionally from learning socialization skills.

Whole books have been written on schizophrenia, so obviously I have not covered the topic in any depth. What I have tried to do is demystify the disorder. Do not use this book and its descriptions of symptoms as a diagnostic tool. If you feel you have any similar symptoms, see a doctor who can make an accurate diagnosis and then give you the help you need.

MANIC DEPRESSION/BIPOLAR DISORDER

Most people have times when they feel down or overexcited; this is a normal part of living. But the person suffering from a bipolar disorder goes to the extremes—from mountainous highs to suicidal lows. When he is high, he is energetic, sometimes aggressive, and more than likely illogical. His thoughts may be jumbled, racing along at ninety miles an hour, or he may be focused on one thought to the exclusion of everything else. Religious preoccupations are not unusual. Teenagers who have experienced these symptoms have later told me that they enjoyed the feelings; unfortunately, the people around them did *not* enjoy the out-of-control behavior, and they are usually the ones who seek treatment for the person.

Persons with this disorder fear the suicidal lows even more than hospitalization. The blackness and terror they feel often prompts them to take their life.

The manic depressive responds to drug therapy, with Lithium being the drug of choice. Lithium seems to bring the two moods together so that the highs are no longer uncontrollable bursts of energy and sleeplessness, and the lows are no longer preludes to suicide. The person may appreciate not having lows, but he usually misses the highs. For that reason, he may stop taking his medicine once his condition has stabilized because he hates the feeling of being "evened out."

Jamie was eighteen when he was first diagnosed with bipolar disorder. He had uncontrollable highs in which he became quite combative, once throwing a chair through a hospital window because he wanted to jump out. His parents could not handle him at home; he couldn't concentrate enough to hold a job; and when he was feeling high he didn't think he *needed* a job.

Jamie was repeatedly hospitalized because whenever he settled down on Lithium he quit taking it. All types of transitional and semi-independent living arrangements were tried, but Jamie lacked the insight to follow through with any treatment plan. Once he withdrew all his savings and hitchhiked across the United States. When his funds ran out in Washington state, he called home for money to get him back to Maine, where he had promised to return to the hospital. But as usual, his grandiose thinking prevented him from seeing the limitations of his illness. Jamie was charming, and as easily charmed by his own carefree behavior as was anyone else. When I last heard from him, he had rejected my latest treatment plan and was moving in with some unsavory character who more than likely wanted the use of Jamie's money (and gullibility).

Marrietta was one of the first teenagers I ever saw who was diagnosed as manic depressive. She was brought onto the ward where I worked and immediately placed in a seclusion room, chiefly for her own safety because her behavior was so offensive to the other patients. Marrietta was full of sexual energy and lay around the seclusion room singing lewd songs and encouraging an audience to form outside. As high as she was, she appeared to be full of drugs, but the opposite was really the case. She resisted taking Lithium because she knew it would bring her down.

Lithium did help her, and within a few days she was more manageable and could talk about her manic episodes. She knew she needed the medicine to level her moods, but she didn't want to give up those highs.

"I get my highs just by being drug-free," she said. "Everyone else has to put something into them. I just sit around and wait for them to happen."

Was she embarrassed later about her behavior when high?

"I know I probably offended a lot of people, but I never hurt anyone; I was just full of energy and having a good time."

It is this kind of illogical thinking that leads to so many relapses. The disorder can be treated—if not with

Lithium (because of medical complications), then with a major tranquilizer. But until the person experiences the other side of the disorder, he may not mind the out-of-control periods.

Marrietta moved out of state after her release from the hospital. A former patient brought us word that a few months after her release Marrietta had quit taking her medicine and during a manic episode had gone swimming and drowned. Apparently she had gone out too far or she had cycled into a depressed state and purposely ended her life.

I have described two cases with unhappy endings, but the prognosis for bipolar disorder is actually quite good. With a good response to medicine and supportive therapists and family, the person can live a normal life. He or she must think of the disorder as like a physical illness such as diabetes that requires continual monitoring. He will never be relieved of the management of the disorder, but despite the care (or rather, because of it) he can live a good life. If he has relapses—even while taking his medicine—chances are that he can head off the most serious problems with brief hospitalizations and get back on course.

DEPRESSION

Being a teenager can be "the pits." You have to deal with all those academic pressures, a body that is playing tricks on you (pimples and other physical disasters), and your struggle to find a direction in life. Not only that, you have to do all this whether your family life is stable or not, and whether or not you have the energy for the tasks. Some people act out their anger about these pressures; other take it out on themselves in the form of depression.

I'm not talking about those times you were upset because you got a D in history or your girlfriend dumped you for a football hero. You felt depressed at the time, and of course, it *was* awful, but you got over it and went on living and struggling and getting into other messes. What I want to talk about are the times when you're so down that you don't even know what's wrong with you and, more significantly, you don't know how to help yourself.

When you're depressed, it is much more than just being down. You may also be anxious. Typically, you have trouble sleeping because your thoughts seem to have taken over your head. All you can do the whole day is think about something (usually bad) over and over again. You don't have the strength to push the bad thought out of your mind. Depressed people have trouble thinking clearly, concentrating, and not acting impulsively. When the symptoms go on long enough, the person loses perspective and no longer knows when he is acting illogically.

Other symptoms that may be easier to spot are the teenager's hopelessness, listlessness, and inability to enjoy anything. When he stops doing things he loves or gives away treasured belongings, he is signaling that he has given up. He can appear to be only half here, as if he has one foot in this world and one in another dimension. I have had people tell me that food no longer had any taste. *These are clinical signs of severe depression* even if not accompanied by suicidal thoughts. Some people never become overtly suicidal; instead they either stay in bed all day, or they act so recklessly that it's as if their body is doing what their mind objects to doing. Having accidents can be a form of suicide.

Sometimes you may know exactly what is bothering you. Major life changes and losses can throw you into depression while you sort out how you can adjust to them. Dorian was a thirteen-year-old girl I saw in the hospital a few years ago. She had tried to kill herself following the death of her sister from leukemia. The scenario seemed right out of the movie "Ordinary People": Dorian was the second-born and the child most often in mischief. Her older sister, Drew, was the apple of her mother's eye. When Drew died following a long, painful illness, Dorian felt guilty for being the one to live. There was a twist to the story, however. Dorian had been abused by her "perfect" older sister, but she was unable to deal with her feelings about that without blaming her dead sister. She could not share the anger and guilt with her mother because her mother was still grieving Drew's loss and Dorian didn't think she would believe her. Torn between her conflicting emotions, Dorian tried to solve the dilemma by ending her own life.

Another girl, Sonya, age sixteen, sought outpatient treatment because of her deep sadness and guilt over the way her life had changed in the past two years. Sonya's parents had divorced, and she had moved to another state with her mother and brother. Her father made no attempt to keep in touch with her. Cut off from all that was familiar, Sonya started behaving promiscuously. When her brother died unexpectedly in a car accident, Sonya gave in to her depression. A colleague saw Sonya for outpatient therapy and helped her look at her pattern of behavior (very similar to other females in her family who had faced unplanned pregnancy, early marriage, marginal income, and minimum-wage jobs). Sonya could finally look at her grief about breaking these familiar patterns and especially going on without some of the people she loved.

But at times teenagers simply do not know why they are depressed or having these terrible, unrelenting thoughts. What they do know is the profound despair they feel, believing that there is no hope and no reason to go on.

These symptoms can be treated. The therapist does not give you hope in the form of a pill, but he does treat the underlying chemical imbalance with antidepressant medication. You do not first have to figure out why you are sad. It is enough to make yourself go to a physician or therapist, because the clinician will recognize the seriousness of your symptoms. It may be hard to believe that medicine can relieve your symptoms. Most people seem to think they have to "get over" their symptoms on their own, but the reality is that you have a biological illness at this point, and willpower alone cannot pull you out of it.

Some people have a wrong idea about prayer. They think that they can lay their symptoms in the hands of God, and He will cure them. You cannot pray to God to take away your symptoms while you do nothing yourself. Prayer is not enough. If God is to help you, you must work together, which means taking responsibility for getting treatment in addition to praying for hope and healing.

In his book *High Times/Low Times*, Dr. John Meeks writes, "Every year two million children between fifteen and nineteen try to kill themselves—and every year some five thousand succeed." Although it is a normal part of adolescence to feel down at times and even to wish you were dead, it is *not* normal to plan your death. If you find yourself thinking that life is too hard for you to go on, you must seek help. When a person is deeply depressed, he or she cannot see how illogically he is thinking. To him, it makes more and more sense to die.

Teenagers worry about a lot of things; after all, the world is a crazier place these days, with the economy in a mess and people's family life less stable than ever. The pressure to succeed is greater today, and the ability to cope may be less.

Other serious conditions called psychosexual disorders

can propel a person into counseling. Teenagers may worry about their sexual identity or the fact that they are attracted sexually to children. As mentioned earlier, it is not normal for children to be sexual partners. If you find yourself wanting close physical contact with a child, you need treatment to help control the impulse. Realizing that you are a "pervert" is demoralizing and depressing.

You might be surprised at how many teenagers struggle with their sexual identity, but for some of you the mere question of being gay may be reason enough to want to end your life. I'm not saying that therapy can alter your sexual leanings; what it can do is give you a place to examine your feelings safely and without censure.

Now that we have discussed some of the disorders, let us see why we came up with these diagnostic categories in the first place. The whole reason for a therapist to diagnose his client is to determine what he is treating. That is also the whole point of writing treatment plans: to enable you and the therapist to know what specific problems need to be worked on in treatment.

Sometimes, however, we find real drawbacks making diagnoses. For one thing, there is danger of seeing the client as a "disorder" instead of a person. In trying to fit a person into a category, the therapist can lose sight of the person and instead treat the symptoms.

Also, a diagnosis is only as good as the person making it. Therapists have been known to tailor a diagnosis so that (1) the young person does not have to be crippled by a "heavy" diagnosis, and (2) the teenager's insurance company will reimburse for the treatment. That should tell you that no diagnosis is written in stone. Some are subject to the whims of their "creators."

Bear in mind, too, that it is possible simply to have some problems, not necessarily symptoms of a greater illness. How severely the problems interfere in your life will influence the type of treatment you choose.

CHAPTER ◇ 5

Where Do You Turn for Help?

If your problems do not seem insurmountable, you might think you can handle them yourself. Self-help books (*How to Get Over the Blues*, *How to Get On with Life*, etc.) give you the author's view of "fixing" things. The disadvantage of reading a book (versus seeing someone) is that you don't really know what the author means. He is not tailoring his advice to your specific situation, and he is not there encouraging you from the sidelines. You have only yourself and the author's unchanging words to guide you.

Self-help books may be a first step in getting treatment or simply acknowledging the problem. The advantage is that you can read them in private, and you don't have to spend money each time you read them. For supportive advice, some of these books are great, but I would caution against using them as blueprints for change. To follow the advice of someone who does not know your circumstances can be dangerous.

Don't misunderstand; books are valuable in giving you ideas. After all, this book is a form of self-help book, although I want you to use it to get the specific treatment you need.

There are other ways to tackle your problems. Your parents, although perhaps not your greatest friends right now, have been through their own adolescent years and might be able to help you. If your problems stem from their abuse, however, obviously you will not want to turn to them, nor would they necessarily be capable of responding to you. Then, too, parents may be so mired in their own problems that they lack the emotional energy or perspective to help you.

Certainly other adults can take the time to listen to you and help you decide on a course of action, Seek out a favorite teacher or a trusted guidance counselor. If you are close to your minister, talk to him or her, bearing in mind, of course, that he will have a religious perspective. He may seem judgmental because of his moral beliefs. But ministers and "men of God" were the original spiritual healers; their job has been usurped by the doctors and psychologists, who have made a point of separating the mind from the spirit.

Ministers are not always qualified to handle psychiatric problems, but they should know when they are out of their depth and refer you to a professional who can work with your disorder.

What role can your friends play? Depending on your symptoms, your friends can be a source of support, either because they have been through similar problems or they are good listeners. Friends have neither the qualifications nor the experience to deal with serious disorders. However, peer support groups have been forming in high schools around the country, demonstrating that peers are sometimes best at getting teenagers to see someone about their problems.

There are limits, of course, to how much another teenager should try to help. Years ago a friend of mine worked as an aide on the ward where I was a social worker. Tom had just graduated from high school and had recently broken up with his girlfriend. He was always morose, but we didn't think much about it because those were morose times. We used to sit around joking about the bleakness of life, but I never meant it when I said I ought to kill myself. Tom meant it. He kept a gun under his bed. Once he showed it to me, and though I hate guns I actually held it and wondered out loud why he kept it around. As winter turned into spring and everyone's mood improved, Tom's got worse. He tried to get me to "do therapy" on him, but I explained that a friend doesn't pretend to be a therapist. I suggested that he see someone, but I didn't give him the name of anyone. Tom hinted that he was having trouble because people thought him gay. Meanwhile, his old girlfriend was getting married.

Tom tried to seduce several of his female coworkers, but none of them were interested in him sexually. He must have taken that as an affront, and if he were worried about his sexual identity their rejection didn't help him.

One night Tom called one of his platonic girlfriends, and they talked for an hour. Tom did not mention any problems, and she thought he was finally coming out of his depression. Tom had made a decision, though. When he hung up the phone he got out his gun and shot himself.

Although I had worked with many suicidal patients, I had never experienced someone's dying. Like his other friends, I felt it was partly my fault. Why had I not heard his pleas for help? Why could I not have taken him more seriously? I could not bring myself to visit his parents after his death because I thought I had let them down too.

Tom got out of his misery, but he left behind a lot of people who are still scarred by his suicide, especially the friend who was the last person to talk with him. She blames herself for letting him down and has been in treatment herself for depression.

Your friends can be a valuable source of support when you are having trouble. They can shore you up with their love and give you reason to keep hanging in there. But they cannot take the place of a trained professional who will know how ill you really are.

Before seeing a therapist, you might first consider seeing your family physician. He or she can run tests to determine whether any physical problems are causing you psychological symptoms. A variety of physical illnesses can cause a person to appear "disturbed." Diabetes, tumors, multiple sclerosis, and even PMS can involve psychiatric difficulties. Even some nutritional deficiencies and certain combinations of drugs (including street drugs and steroids) can account for someone's acting "crazy." Don't reach for a medical encyclopedia and look for a medical condition to account for your symptoms; see your doctor.

Not every problem can be solved with one pat answer or even one specific form of treatment. Sometimes it is a matter of seeing what help is available and choosing the course of action that best fits your needs. If you decide to involve professionals, they might recommend outpatient counseling, hospitalization, or a combination of both. They might suggest a group home if your problems cannot be managed in your parents' house.

Group homes are structured living environments where kids learn to fit into society by modifying their behavior. Dr. Robert Allanach, Executive Director of Western

Maine Institute for Psychotheraphy and Education, has established the Western Maine Children's Center in Bridgton as a home for emotionally disordered boys ages eight to twelve. He offers it as a "place to feel safe." This group home differs from others, he says, in that it offers:

1. Clearly defined boundaries for the boys.
2. Clearly defined rules with clearly defined punishments for breaking the rules.
3. A homey atmosphere instead of institutional living.
4. A place where kids learn to do things differently.

Any group home is only as good as its staff and especially its director. If the people in charge believe that a person can change if given love, guidance, and incentive (which is where peer pressure comes in), the conduct-disordered youngster has a chance to change the course of his life before he is irretrievably lost in the legal system.

Lastly, alternatives to professional treatment of your problems do exist. Drugs, alcohol, and promiscuity are all ways people use to avoid dealing with the real problems. Drugs and alcohol are escapist; you drink or pop pills to push away the pain. It may work for a while, but then the problems come back and you have another one—substance abuse—on top of them.

Some teenagers use behavior to distract attention from their problems. Being promiscuous—thinking a lot of guys find you desirable—works to counteract those horrible feelings of worthlessness. If someone is loving you—even if he is only using you to gratify his own needs—it is easier to believe you are lovable (even if your parents have abandoned you). The problem with that, however, is that you may wind up with a baby and no husband, and believe me, that baby will not realize it is here to meet *your* needs for love and acceptance. Nor will those temporary lovers change the fact that your parents deserted you, physically or emotionally. You will not find parental love with a sexually irresponsible young man.

Keeping your teachers or the police at their wits' end is not going to take the spotlight long off your problems, either. If you are agonizing over mistreatment at home or your parents' divorce, changing the focus to your lying and stealing at school will only complicate the situation. And you will not necessarily feel better at having gotten back at your parents, because they are not going to figure out that you're lying and stealing because you're mad at *them*. It takes a strong person to be able to look at his or her problems squarely *and do something constructive about them*. It is not a cop-out to ask for professional help.

CHAPTER ◇ 6

Outpatient Therapy

Before you decide what is supposed to go on in a therapy session, you must find a reputable therapist. Where do you look?

Selecting a good therapist is not necessarily a matter of money; some reputable therapists work in clinics, where they base their fees on the person's ability to pay. Having your sessions in an agency setting does not mean that your privacy will be compromised. I doubt that the town gossips hang out around mental health agencies, waiting to see who comes and goes.

Nowadays therapy sessions cost from $60 to $120 an hour, depending on the city and the therapist. If the therapist is licensed and you have insurance coverage, you can expect to be reimbursed for all or part of the cost. If your family does not have health insurance, you can look in the phone book under "Family Services and Counseling" or "Mental Health" for the nearest community mental health agency or counseling service. These places charge on a sliding scale according to how much money you or your family make.

Perhaps you are confused about the type of therapist

you should see. Would a psychiatrist, a psychologist, or a social worker help you most?

There *are* differences among therapists, but not necessarily the ones you might think of. Of course, the backgrounds differ for the several professions, but more important than that, the therapists themselves will differ in their attitudes and their ability to relate to you. Finding a therapist with whom you are comfortable is more important than whether he or she is a psychologist or a social worker.

As I said, there are differences in background and training emphasis for each of these professionals. A psychiatrist is the only one who can prescribe medicine. He earns a medical degree and goes on to specialize in psychiatry, so that he knows both the body and the mind. Someone with an emotional disorder that requires medication would need to see either a psychiatrist or a therapist who works with one. The fact that a psychiatrist is at the top of the profession does not mean that he is the best person to work with you on your problems. He may be, but he may also have less time for you and certainly will cost substantially more.

A psychologist is someone with a degree in Clinical Psychology (PhD) or Counseling and Education (EdD). This person cannot prescribe medication. He or she will have gone to a four-year college and then spent four to five more years at the graduate level. Just as the psychiatrist belongs to professional organizations to monitor his behavior, so does the psychologist. An advantage of the psychologist is that he or she can administer educational or personality tests and interpret the results.

The clinical social worker is a trained counselor who has a graduate degree (MSW or DSW), requiring two to four years of school beyond a four-year college. Clinical social workers often specialize in treating certain clients such as victims of abuse, or troubled families, or Vietnam veterans. Social workers typically know the resources in the community, which is an additional strength in working with the troubled client. A licensed social worker can belong to the National Association of Social Workers. Like his or her licensed counterparts, the nurse, the psychologist, and the psychiatrist, the social worker attends workshops or schools for continuing educational credits and to keep abreast of the latest findings and theories in mental health.

The psychiatric nurse or nurse clinician is both a regular nurse (having either an RN license or a BS degree in nursing) and a clinician, additionally trained in psychology (psychiatric nursing or counseling). Like the other professionals, he or she must pass licensing exams and undergo a period of supervision to ensure that he is qualified to practice. The nurse clinician also belongs to professional organizations.

Of course, others are trained to work with troubled persons, but without licensing you have little recourse should they abuse your trust.

Don't be swayed by fancy diplomas or Ivy League schools. Heavy credentials do not guarantee a good working relationship or a successful outcome of treatment. More than anything else it means that *a lot of money was spent on the person's education*.

Once you have found a reputable agency, you will be given an intake appointment. In this initial session the therapist (who is not necessarily the one who will work with you after this first appointment) will want to know what brought you to the agency in order to help you decide on the next course of action. (Should you also see the staff psychiatrist? Should family sessions be scheduled instead of or in addition to individual sessions?)

By the way, family sessions are not designed to spread the anguish around. In some cases, seeing the whole family prevents the ailing family from scapegoating the member with the identified problem. Therapists do not seek to decide who is the real culprit. Rather they try to examine the relationships within the family, noting the strengths of each member and the alliances and how things seem to be going wrong. Even when only one person seems to be showing "the problem," there are symptoms of stress in all members. The goal is to treat the entire family system.

One of your first hurdles may be getting yourself to go to therapy. A young girl once told me she went to therapy only because her mother made her go. She had nothing she wanted to tell the therapist because as she saw it, "It was none of the therapist's business!" Kerry displayed some of the old Yankee attitude—that a person must live with and deal with her problems herself, that you are not supposed to burden others with your problems.

In the early days of this country it was probably necessary to solve your own problems. Living in the wilderness, you had no neighbors with whom to discuss something bothering you. Nor did you have time to talk when your very existence depended on your working from dawn to dusk. But we don't live in those times anymore. And in discussing your personal problems with a professional, you have not given up responsibility for them. What a therapist aims to do is help *you* to find the answers, for the answers lie within you. But to accomplish that, he or she must be the right therapist.

What *are* the qualities of a good therapist? First of all, the good therapist is someone you can trust. You can trust her to take your problem seriously and treat you with respect—which means not hearing her later laughing with the receptionist about that kid who came in complaining about her parents.

The good therapist knows about boundaries. He or she knows that he cannot be a friend to a client and also his therapist. You cannot meet for tennis lessons and then face off in the therapy room once a week. Likewise, a therapist does not date a client. *Sexual relations between therapist and client are* unethical and illegal. The client has come to the therapist for help, not to be further victimized. Any reputable therapist knows this rule and will not initiate sex with you. If he does, you must stop seeing him immediately, and you should report him to his agency or licensing board.

It is not unusual to be sexually attracted to your therapist or for him or her to be attracted to you. You simply do not act on the feelings. A sexual relationship changes the nature of the therapeutic relationship. No longer are you partners in working through a problem.

Sometimes the boundaries about touching are fuzzy. Dwain will not initiate hugs with his clients because hugs are so often misinterpreted. If someone asks him for a hug, which has happened, he may comply but will ask the client why she thinks she needed it. Sometimes it is because a client—particularly one who has grown accustomed to using her sexuality to cement relationships—wants to change the focus of his feelings. Other times the client simply wants to crawl into his lap and be babied. But a therapist is not a parent, and touching cannot be used to avoid dealing with the real problem, whatever it may be.

When I was terminating therapy sessions with my clients before moving to Maine, I bought them each a copy of the book *One Morning in Maine*. At our last session I gave it to them along with a hug if they seemed to want one. I was aware that hugging—physically touching each other—would produce strong feelings in both of us. One woman, Ellen, said at the outset of our session that she did not want to hug me good-bye.

"It'll just make me cry," she said. "And I'm not going to cry at this last session."

"Okay," I said, "I won't give you a hug. But is it so awful to cry about my leaving?"

"I cry too much as it is," she said. "I don't want to cry anymore."

"Are you mad at me for leaving and going so far away? I mean, it's not as if Maine were right around the corner, you know."

We spent the rest of the time talking about my leaving and how abandoned she felt even though we had arranged for her to continue with another therapist at the agency. At the end of the hour Ellen said, "I still don't want that hug."

I gave her the book and said, "Well, I'll walk you to the lobby, then."

I wished her well and actually felt sad that she hadn't allowed me to give her the hug.

Halfway out the door, Ellen turned. "Oh, what the hell," she said, and threw her arms around me. Then, as predicted, she cried, but by then we were both misty-eyed, so it didn't matter.

Touching releases powerful emotions. The good therapist knows how to handle them.

People accuse therapists of "just doing their job—not really caring." It's true; counseling people *is* their job, and they are paid for it. Nonetheless, therapists cannot enter into so personal a relationship without feeling something for the client. It is also their job, however, not to let personal feelings get in the way of work.

Sometimes you may feel overwhelmed by your emotions in working with a therapist. You may put up barriers, seeking either to protect yourself from getting too close or to slow the process of dealing with your troubles. Most therapists will accept your resistance and allow you to work at your own pace, even understanding your need every so often to withdraw from treatment. Remember, the therapist does not hold the answers to your problems; at best, the two of you work together to solve them.

The good therapist keeps what you say confidential. Within reason. It you report any kind of abuse, by law the therapist must report that information to the Department of Human Services. Dwain makes agreements at the outset of treating adolescents. If they are to work together in therapy, they must agree to his "rules":

1. If you tell me you're planning to do something dangerous, or that I consider to be dangerous, I will inform your parents or guardian.
2. If your parents inquire how you are doing, I will say. "Fine" but not go into specifics.
3. If I have reason to meet with your parents, I will tell you the content of our discussions, or we can arrange joint meetings.

Without the client's or his parent's permission, Dwain will not discuss the client's case.

Therapists sometimes have a client sign a contract, particularly if the client is suicidal. A contract typically states that the client agrees to contact the therapist before acting on any impulse. The therapist makes this arrangement not to have full control over the teenager's life, but to be involved in the teenager's life. On occasion a suicidal teenager needs the therapist to keep him from hurting himself or others.

Therapists have different styles and personalities, so naturally some will work better with you than others. Some do a lot of talking; others sit back and let you do the talking. Some even make jokes. Be careful to find one who is not judgmental or overly critical. Not all therapists are nonjudgmental, even though they are supposed to be. A woman I know was sexually abused by her brother for years. When the abuse came to light, the woman's mother sent her to a psychiatrist. The psychiatrist was an older man who perhaps had not dealt with issues of this nature. Essentially he told the young woman that having endured the situation for years, she must have enjoyed it to some degree and therefore was not in a position to fault her brother completely. Fortunately, the woman left treatment, because the psychiatrist was perpetuating a myth. The victim is never responsible, and he or she has a right to his feelings. The point of therapy is for the person to own his or her feelings, not for the therapist to point the finger of blame.

Sometimes new therapists are quick to offer advice. Remember, you are not in therapy to get a quick cure. The purpose of therapy is to find the solutions *yourself* with the guidance and help of a professional, not for the therapist to impress you with his knowledge.

How long do people stay in treatment? Some people who consider themselves professional clients (like Woody Allen) may be in treatment all their lives. But usually treatment is relatively short-term. Depending on the nature of your problem, you might see a therapist once a week (in fifty-minute sessions) for several months. Working through issues of abuse may take more than a year. People with chronic disorders needing long-term management may expect to be in some form of treatment for years, but not necessarily fifty-minute sessions once a week.

Perhaps after reading all this you're thinking, "Can't a person get better without any kind of treatment?"

Again, the answer depends. Some people would get better if you sat them in a room with a therapist who read the phone book with them. Their own belief that they were "doing something" would account for most of their improvement. My colleague and friend, Sondra Shehab, expressed it best. She wrote me that probably some of the adolescents she has seen would have gotten better without any intervention, but "treatment shortened the suffering and allowed them to get on with their lives. Often, treatment helps a kid know that he/she has a *right* to a life."

Sometimes in his private practice Dwain has encountered people "shopping around" for a therapist. The client would talk for a while about what was bothering him and then say, "All right, how will you handle this?" as if it were a contest and the first therapist to give the "right" answer would "win" this guy as a client.

Sometimes clients stay with Dwain long enough for him to say something they don't like to hear, and they immediately quit treatment in search of another therapist who will say something more to their liking. Therapy is hard work. You should not make a snap decision about a therapist based on one or two sessions. Give individual therapy a trial of five or six sessions before quitting, and always be straight with the therapist about why you are leaving. With group therapy, give yourself eight or more sessions before deciding against it. You need the additional sessions to get a perspective on whether or not the people in the group, not to mention the therapists themselves, can help you.

You may be thinking, "Well, if therapists don't give advice and don't have any answers, why am I bothering to go to them in the first place?"

Believe me, you are not the first person to have thought of that question. The fact that therapists do not give you advice does not mean that they are not doing anything for you. They are just wise enough to keep their mouth shut and their ears open. At best, they can point you in the direction you want to grow. They can help untangle your emotions and point out incidents of bad judgment. Then, too, with serious problems they know when to refer to a doctor for medication or hospitalization.

Therapy is a painful process whereby the client usually gets better by first getting worse. Whenever you start looking at the pain in your life, you are going to feel *bad*. Unfortunately you have to dig through all that pain before you can get out from under it. The temptation is to quit therapy when the going gets rough, but the problem with that is that you'll be stuck in the middle of all your pain. You no doubt already know that *problems don't just evaporate when you stop looking at them*.

Some people play games in therapy as a way to keep from looking at the problem or to avoid intimacy with the therapist. Remember, the therapist is on *your* side. It is not an adversarial relationship.

A lawyer friend of Dwain's once told us that he could outtalk either of us in therapy sessions.

"You may be right," I said, "but who would be the loser?"

Clients have come to therapy sessions high on marijuana. One guy then blamed his therapist—and quit—on the ground that the therapist could not be very smart if he had not noticed that the client was stoned.

I'm not going to tell you not to play games, because any therapist worth his salt will call you on it. We know resistance when we see it, even when it takes the form of clients bringing us presents before each session.

I guess I still haven't told you what goes on behind those closed doors. Sometimes you just sit and talk about what is bothering you—even the fact that you're mad at the therapist for being late for your appointment. But therapists relate to their clients in other ways that are still considered therapy. Sometimes the therapist serves as a role model, particularly with clients who come from chaotic backgrounds and need someone stable in their life to model their own growing up on. Sometimes the therapist "plays" with children because the very young child is not always able to verbalize his feelings. An associate of mine worked with an eight-year-old firebug who could not possibly tell her why he set fires. Ginny let him play with some Fisher Price dolls and a playhouse, and his turmoil at home came tumbling out of the dolls.

Dwain also does what we call "Dutch-uncling," which is a form of modeling. He takes the client out into the community. Sometimes he takes him to the video arcade and simply plays games—or so it seems. Actually, he is building a relationship with the client, who is learning socialization skills: how to behave in public and how to trust Dwain to help him with other problems. Sometimes, Dwain plays cards with his younger clients, or Frisbee if the weather is right. It's hard to explain to our kids what Daddy does for work when we drive by his office and see him out on the lawn playing Frisbee with some little kid.

Problems do come up in therapy. Sometimes when you are working through particularly bad memories and experiences you suddenly find yourself "falling apart." The therapist, for the most part, can keep you from coming totally unglued, but sometimes he can't stop what we call "decompensating." Some people become suicidal again, or so confused that they can't make any decisions because of the stress of what they have been working on. At such a point the therapist may recommend inpatient treatment (because of the safer environment) while continuing to work on the painful issues, or else taking a break from such in-depth work.

When a crisis occurs—such as the phone call in the night when the client threatens to kill himself—the therapist stops being the inactive role model and actively steps in to take care of you. He may call the police or demand that your relatives take you to the hospital. Whatever the scenario, the relationship with the therapist is forever altered. The therapist has actively intervened, possibly breaking the client's trust by involving other agencies to help him. That represents a crisis not only for the client, but for the therapist himself, who may have feelings of anger and helplessness about the situation. It will take time to work through those feelings as well.

A word to the wise: Therapy is not meant to be a place where you go to rationalize your current behavior by blaming it all on a "bad childhood." I was trying to figure out how to put that message across when I heard Data on a recent "Star Trek" episode advising another person, "*Your past does not excuse you from immoral or unethical behavior*."

"Perfect," I thought. "I couldn't have said it better!"

Finally, realize the limits of therapy. No therapist can instill good judgment in someone who does not have the capacity for it. A therapist cannot make a conduct-disordered person become a model citizen, although he can help modify that conduct if the person is willing. And no matter what you want treatment for, you cannot get unconditional love from the therapist as if he were your new parent.

A girl I once knew was in treatment for depression related to a background of severe parental "disregard"; I wouldn't have called it abuse. One day in the middle of a session she looked at me and said, "You know, it just hit me. I think what I've really been coming here for was to get your approval. As if I could undo all that has happened to me by getting you to like me. I mean, I know I can't go back and get my own folks to love me like a little kid again. But I guess I thought if I could get you to like me—well, maybe I could get all that unconditional stuff from *you*."

"And?" I asked.

"And what just hit me from out of the blue is that I probably can't get that from you, and even if I could, you aren't my parents, so it wouldn't be the same. What I want is for you to make me into someone that my parents will love so that *then* I can get the unconditional love I still want."

"I can't make you into that person," I said.

"I know," she said. "And that's why I'm so sad right now. I know I'll *never* get that stuff. And it hurts."

"I think you're going to get better now," I said.

"I think I *am* better now," she said.

Sometimes, as you can see, the clients have something to teach the therapist...

CHAPTER ◇ 7

Hospitalization

Just as there are different kinds of outpatient therapy, inpatient facilities are varied. Before admitting yourself or letting anyone else admit you, consider all your choices. For adolescent disorders in which you are not violent, dangerous to yourself, or likely to run away, you might consider going to a "regular" hospital that has a psychiatric wing. Hospitals in this category vary in policies, but as a rule, you need insurance coverage to be treated.

If you have a psychiatrist on the outside, he will more than likely have hospital privileges that will allow him to continue to treat you. If your therapist is a social worker or psychologist, he or she may have custodial privileges, which allow him or her to treat you in conjunction with a psychiatrist. Often the therapist knows a psychiatrist who has hospital privileges, and they coordinate their treatment.

At some hospitals, even though you have a therapist on the outside, you will receive treatment from the doctors and social workers on the ward to which you have been assigned. They will attempt to coordinate your care with your outpatient therapist so that you can resume treatment with him or her when you leave the hospital.

If you do not have a therapist and are hospitalized for the first time, you will be assigned the on-call psychiatrist. The psychiatrist you meet in the emergency room will follow you on the psychiatric ward, or you will be assigned to a team of the next available doctor, social worker, and nurse. The social worker you see on the psychiatric ward can also help you make connections with outpatient services when you start making plans for discharge.

The length of psychiatric hospitalization varies with the disorder and the person manifesting it. You might be hospitalized as long as thirty days (which coincides with the maximum length of stay that most insurance companies cover), but you may recover more quickly. Staffers should be careful not to use up unnecessarily your allotted days of inpatient treatment, because you might not be eligible for further insured hospitalization for another calendar year.

Advantages of treatment in this type of setting are the continuity of care with your outpatient therapist and the lesser stigma associated with being in a "regular" hospital. A drawback may be that the staff is not as well prepared to deal with a psychotic person or one requiring special attention.

Community mental health centers with inpatient facilities are another good place of treatment because of their shorter hospitalizations and more relaxed atmosphere. Remember, though, that all facilities reflect their staff's temperament, so some may be less relaxed than others.

The Mental Health Center where Dwain and I worked in Oklahoma had an inpatient section housing a variety of patients with different disorders and degrees of difficulty. Some patients were kept on the unit at all times; others could come and go on the grounds to meals (where everyone ate together, including the staff) and to activities. If someone was considered dangerous or could not handle this less-structured environment, he was transferred to the state hospital in the same town. Patients usually stayed a maximum of thirty days at the Center, although they might continue treatment in partial hospitalization programs for months after that. Another benefit of the comprehensive mental health center is that one can receive a variety of services at the same facility. For someone who had been hospitalized at the Center, it was less confusing—more reassuring—to be followed up on an outpatient basis at the same location. And finally it was far less stigmatizing to have been hospitalized at the Mental Health Center than at the state hospital right around the corner.

Private psychiatric hospitals usually set aside a wing that specifically treats adolescents with emotional disorders. In general, those people under the age of eighteen are considered adolescents. Specialized psychiatric hospitals vary in their approach to treatment. Some focus on the social component of the illness, using a behavioral approach (with rules and punishments) to deal with inappropriate symptoms. Other hospitals see the teenager's disorder as a blend of biological illness (requiring medication) and social stresses; therefore treatment is aimed both at the biological illness and at reducing the stress in the environment.

Like all facilities, some are good and some not so good: those staffed by people who believe that "bad things happen to good people" and those staffed by people who believe that "people get what they deserve."

For the teenager, a real concern is to arrive at a place whose staff either doesn't understand or doesn't *like* adolescents. Federal funds have been devoted to special programs for the treatment of adolescents, so naturally we have seen an increase in facilities. Insurance companies spend more money each year on adolescents; the same teens who formerly might have been seen as suffering the pangs of growing up are now treated in hospitals for problems labeled emotional disorders.

Realize that adolescent admissions to psychiatric units are on the increase, which does not necessarily mean that more and more adolescents are in need of inpatient treatment. It may mean that that is where the money and interest are. On the other hand, these private hospitals do provide the teenager with a structured environment where he or she can work on problems safely.

In some towns you can be admitted to separate children's facilities where you live, receive therapy (usually only for emotional disturbances, not for psychotic conditions), and attend school. If you are under the age allowed to quit school legally, you will be expected to attend classes either in the hospital or in one-to-one tutorial sessions. Such children's centers receive an enormous amount of state and federal funds because they aim to save the child before he is too old.

Lastly, there are the state hospitals. I say lastly because I hope they are your last resort. State hospitals are notoriously staffed by underpaid and underqualified people. As you can guess, people who are unhappy in their job or do not feel appreciated by the higher-ups will not do their best. If they are actually not qualified for their job, it won't matter if they do their best because their best will not be adequate. Although state hospitals attract their share of idealistic, concerned people, their low pay and poor incentives do little toward keeping those people.

What does that mean for you? Well, put simply, staff that are not qualified to take care of you or *are not happy* taking care of you will be doing a poor job. Stressed by time, low energy, and a million other demands, they will not be able to give you the attention you need. When I was a graduate student working as an aide in a state hospital I believed that sometimes people got well in spite of us, rather than because of us.

Treatment costs vary, with the private facilities, of course, costing the most. Insurance companies have liberal policies on treating adolescents these days, so your parents should check their policies before assuming that treatment is too costly. Sometimes private hospitals have "free beds," a certain number of beds allocated to people who can't afford to pay anything toward treatment. With that in mind, never assume that you will be refused admission because of inability to pay.

Confidentiality is a moot point for those of you under eighteen. Technically, your parents or guardians sign you into a hospital, and hence they should by law have access to your records. In actuality, most staff are sensitive to patient-doctor confidentiality and will involve your parents in joint meetings with you rather than private conferences. On the other hand, if you do something dangerous on the unit you can bet your parents will hear about it.

Where you ultimately go for inpatient treatment may depend on other factors such as what is available in your area. Should you go to the state hospital in your town because your family will be able to visit you every few days? Or should you pool the family resources and go to a place out of state where you will receive first-rate care but see your family less often? Those are things to consider.

One last word about hospitals: Don't admit yourself to a psychiatric hospital to avoid the law. In some places, if you have committed a crime you cannot even receive services until the charges have been disposed of. Psychiatric hospitals are not meant to house criminals, and few psychiatrists are either prepared or have the time to decide whether a person was "crazy" and in need of psychiatric care when he committed a crime.

A teenager recently made an appointment to see Dwain. Although the girl had been charged with shoplifting, she displayed no remorse. In fact, when Dwain asked what had brought her into treatment, she said, "My lawyer thought it would be a good idea if I came here. It might look good in court."

"So what do you need treatment for?" Dwain asked her.

"Well, I don't know," the girl answered.

Remember, if you cannot delineate your problem and you have been charged with an offense, a hospital will not allow itself to be used to get you out of trouble. You don't need treatment; you need to face the music.

CHAPTER ◇ 8

Voluntary Admission

I was watching the evening news recently and saw a segment on mental health care for adolescents. According to the report, adolescent psychiatric admissions were up by 450 percent in the last decade, and whereas in the past doctors had treated severe emotional disorders, increasingly they were now admitting adolescents suffering the problems of "growing up." I thought about my work at Jackson Brook Institute, and I wondered if the adolescents I had seen there had only been suffering adjustment reactions.

It has been four years since I worked at the hospital, but I still remember my surprise at the severity of illness in the young people we treated. Perhaps other hospitals are seeing more teenagers who can handle their problems in a less restrictive way, but the teens I saw were invariably in a crisis.

When I took my turn working in Admissions, I always

considered first whether the adolescent was dangerous (in other words, did he or she need so structured an environment?), whether he or she had any support outside the hospital, and what were the environmental stresses. It was of little use to us as clinicians to work with teenagers who represented little threat to themselves or others and who clearly did not think they had any problems.

Let me tell you what an ordinary admission procedure was like back then, bearing in mind, of course, that there is no such thing as an "ordinary" anything.

When a person came in for admission, he or she was usually accompanied by a parent or guardian (because some adult responsible for the person had to sign the admission papers). The parent or guardian had usually already talked with the Admissions people about the likelihood of admission, the cost, and the availability of beds. As the social worker on duty, I made an initial assessment of the teenager. I preferred to have everyone present at first to hear what the problems at home (or school) were. If the teenager was reluctant to talk with the parents present, I asked the parents to wait outside while I spoke with the teenager alone. Mostly what I was looking for was whether the teenager herself thought she had a problem serious enough to require hospitalization. If she seemed to have enough insight and support at home, I might decide that the problems could be handled on an outpatient basis. But if the teenager was dangerous (either wanting to hurt herself or someone else) or needed medication, I opted for admission—and always planned on a short stay. If medication was to be introduced, it would take ten days to two weeks to be effective.

Assuming that I did not have to persuade the teenager to sign in to the hospital, I explained about the therapy programs we offered and invited the parents back to discuss their involvement with the teenager. We did not want to separate the teen from her parents because after hospitalization they were going to have to get back together anyway. It was better to start the getting-along process while the teenager was in the hospital.

When I had determined that the teenager was a candidate for admission (or even if I were not sure), I called in the psychiatrist on duty, who listened to my observations, asked questions of his own, and then decided with me on the best course of treatment. If it were to be admission to the hospital, the doctor took a quick history of the patient, and she was taken to be oriented to the ward.

If you are the teenager in need of hospitalization, you are still considered a voluntary admission even if you do not want to be in the hospital. *The fact that your parents sign you in* makes you a voluntary admission.

Peggy was fourteen and having all sorts of problems with her folks. Actually they were her adoptive parents, and the friction had begun when they adopted her at the age of five. Peggy said she never fit with them, and the "fit" only got worse when she hit junior high school. For months they had tried outpatient therapy, but Peggy was determined not to say anything in the sessions, which further antagonized her folks. The angrier they were, the more Peggy withdrew. Perhaps she didn't even know what was bugging her. In any event, she continued to have trouble in school and with any authority figure who crossed her path.

One day Peggy had had enough and climbed over the protective fence surrounding a bridge in town. She was going to jump into the river.

A passing motorist stopped in the middle of the bridge, raced over, and plucked Peggy from her perch above the water. Not knowing what to do with her, and because

Peggy was angry rather than relieved, the man took her to the police station. Peggy's parents were not pleased to hear of her latest escapade and suggested that the police take her to the nearest hospital. Later that evening the hospital requested that the police transfer Peggy to a private psychiatric hospital in a neighboring town.

When Peggy came in to the Admissions office, she was wearing handcuffs because she had threatened to run away. Given that she had no place to go and was a suicidal risk, she was admitted. As a voluntary admission. Her parents, who showed up for the procedure, signed her in.

But the good thing about voluntary status is that you can leave when you want as long as you are not a danger to yourself or others. You can request to leave in writing and your request must be honored as long as your parents or guardians will accompany you.

But let's assume that you want to be hospitalized and are willing to have your parents sign you in. What can you expect to happen now?

A clinician will be assigned to your case. This therapist will be a psychologist, a social worker, or a clinical nurse. He or she will be responsible for coordinating all aspects of your treatment and seeing that you receive any necessary psychological or neurological testing or physicals. He or she will be your primary therapist, providing your individual therapy and arranging family meetings. The psychiatrist will monitor your overall care, but he or she usually delegates the day-to-day treatment to your clinician and the nursing staff. A rotating shift of nurses and aides will follow you closely on the ward. Well, let me rephrase that. They won't as a rule follow you around unless specific orders are written for them to keep you under constant supervision. But the nursing staff will be the most familiar faces you see, next to the other patients, of course. Depending on what your problems are, the nursing staff may do bloodwork on you, check your vital signs periodically, and at best spend time just talking with you.

Most hospitals emphasize group therapy, because peer groups are more productive encounters. You may think it is easy to con an adult; it's much harder to con someone who has the same outlook on life and the same problems you have. Group therapy sessions are an important way teenagers realize their impact on each other.

Adolescents (as well as some adults) commonly complain that the groups are boring or not useful—or both at once. If the groups are boring, you have to share part of the responsibility for that. Haven't your parents ever told you that you get out of something just what you put into it? By denying that therapy is of any use to you, you protect your secrets a little longer, but what have you gained? You won't get better by guarding your pain.

Individual therapy sessions, where you spend anywhere from fifteen to forty-five minutes with your primary therapist, are good for getting you committed to therapy. Making contact with a specific person who devotes time to you and your problems is an important first step. Sometimes it is easier to talk about your problems with only one other person in the room.

Another therapeutic activity you will be expected to attend is occupational therapy, which most teenagers associate with crafts. Its purpose is to give the person an alternate way to express his feelings; for example, pounding clay may be the safest way for a teen to express pent-up rage at his father. Also occupational therapy gives the person something productive to do—a new skill to master, a lifelong hobby. Time on a hospital unit is rigidly structured so that the patient does not have hours to spend alone with his or her problems.

Recreational therapy involves physical exercise, so many teenagers come to associate RT with "playing." Not so. There is a method to all that ball-throwing and running. Some people have to wear themselves out physically before they can get to the root of their problems. Others may get so worn out from working on their problems that they need some diversion, and structured play is productive diversion. Then, too, games stress cooperation and competition, skills that all of us have to master to get along in society.

I remember once when our group therapy sessions were going nowhere, Ginny (my associate) and I decided to take the group outside to play a game of volleyball. Ginny and I changed into sneakers and took off our jackets. Then we trooped outside and lined up on opposite sides of the net. Suddenly those very patients who had had nothing to talk about in group were yelling instructions and encouragement to each other, and Ginny and I were jumping all over the lawn trying to keep the volleyball in the air. In the end, after we were all worn out from the play, we had probably communicated better with our patients than in all of our other group therapy sessions combined. Sometimes the focus of therapy needs to shift simply to relating to others. And to do that, sometimes you just need to play.

Ideally, your family will not desert you upon admission. The staff wants to keep the family involved in your treatment because you will probably be living with them upon discharge, and besides, problems don't exist in a vacuum. What has been happening to you—your depression, anxiety, excitability—has been affecting your family, too.

It helps for them to be able to work on the stress at home while you are still in the hospital and not directly in the middle of the mess.

What if your family does abandon you?

If you cannot return to your family, for whatever reason, the hospital staff works to find you another home. You would never be turned loose to fend for yourself.

A hospital is not meant to be a vacation spa, so you are not supposed to be having "the time of your life." At best, it is a safe place where people who can help you with your emotions are around you all the time. But volunteering to live there temporarily means that you agree to follow a few rules. You may not smash up the place, even if you have little control over your emotions. If you do go on a rampage or tantrum, know that the staff will intervene to prevent your hurting yourself, others, or their property.

How will they do that?

Depending on the circumstances, staff members will either talk you out of your behavior or physically restrain you (without purposely hurting you in the process). As a last resort, they may give you medication to calm you down. Now that I have brought up the subject of drugs, I might as well digress for a few minutes.

Why do doctors prescribe drugs?

First of all, you have to accept that every illness has two parts. One is the biological component, the actual physical illness, that has produced the symptoms. The other is the psychosocial component, the part that reflects the months and years of stress in your family and other relationships from dealing with these symptoms. Doctors use medication if they think there is a biological basis for your problems. With some depressions, it is not a matter of "willing" yourself out of the dumps. Scientists have discovered genuine chemical imbalances in the brain that account for mood disturbance. Although you may gain some relief from a hospital stay and being away from familial stresses for the time being, you might see faster relief with an antidepressant medication. Understand that these medications are not addictive. The person taking them does not get "high" and does not need to increase the dosage down the line in order to get the same effect. Dosage may fluctuate over time depending on body weight and levels of stress, but not because the person has become addicted and needs a larger dose.

Not all clinicians believe in medicating adolescents. Some people believe that they should learn to get over their problems without relying on chemicals, even prescribed medications. But that is like saying that teenagers with juvenile diabetes should not take insulin because their body will just get used to it and require it. If you think of symptoms as having a *physical* basis, you can better appreciate why doctors introduce drugs.

Doctors use medication to treat the physical symptoms, but they still provide therapy to treat the psychosocial component of the illness. You can take an antidepressant to lift your mood, but without supportive therapy you will not understand what has been going wrong in your life, nor how to muster your own emotional strength. Therapy is designed to give you the insight and impetus to change and to help you capitalize on your strengths.

In an earlier chapter I discussed the medications used and some of the side effects. As a voluntary patient you have the right to refuse any treatment, which, of course, includes medication. Understand, however, that if your behavior presents a threat to anyone—including yourself—you can be medicated against your will.

Peggy, who you may remember was admitted to the hospital on a voluntary basis even though she did not want to be there, got into a few free-for-alls on her ward. On more than one occasion she was given a shot of Thorazine to sedate her, after which she eventually calmed down. She later told me that she and the other adolescents fought as much as they did in order to get "shot up with Thorazine."

"Now why would you want Thorazine shots?" I asked.

"Because you can get high off them," she said.

She must have been right, because she obviously liked the effects enough to seek them over and over again. Thorazine would not have been my drug of choice; with some people who do not need the drug, it can induce hallucinations. And prolonged or heavy use of this potent medication causes uncomfortable side effects: blurred vision, dry mouth, and involuntary facial and hand movements. It is not a drug to play around with, nor is it a way to control your behavior on the outside.

Back to the subject of "rights": You do not necessarily retain all of them even though you are a voluntary patient. Your telephone privileges may be curtailed, your right to come and go freely on the grounds may be restricted, and your sexual life will definitely be restricted. (The belief is that you've got enough to work on without adding any sexual problems, unplanned pregnancies or complicating relationships.)

The rights you do retain vary from one hospital to the next, as does the amount of supervision you receive. Nonetheless, you still have more rights than if you were involuntarily committed to the hospital, which involves the courts, the police, and a lot of unwillingness on your part. In the next chapter we shall look at what happens if you end up in a hospital against your will.

Remember, though, no matter how you end up in a hospital, *you always have the right to be treated with dignity and respect.*

CHAPTER ◇ 9

Involuntary Commitment

Usually when a teenager is hospitalized against her will, she is still considered a voluntary admission because her parents sign her in. There are occasions, however, when a parent won't sign the teenager into a hospital, and the adolescent becomes an involuntary patient if need be. Involuntary status is more significant for adults because they have more recourse to protest their admission. Sometimes teenagers have to suffer the decision of their parents. So although I talk about involuntary status in this chapter, you can consider any time a teenager is hospitalized against her will as applying here.

Recently, Dwain evaluated a young girl in the emergency room of the hospital. She was confused and hallucinating and needed to be in a psychiatric hospital for her own safety. Her mother, who accompanied her to the emergency room, would not sign papers for her daughter to be admitted. She was afraid the girl would hate her for "signing her away," as she put it. With no family member willing to sign the girl in, Dwain and the emergency room staff had to pursue an involuntary commitment. The girl was suicidal—the more so because of her obvious confusion and hallucinations. Because she was a clear risk to herself, commitment papers could be filed on her. A doctor must affirm on commitment papers that the person is in immediate need of hospitalization. The sheriff's office (or the police) can transport the person to the hospital. Within a specified period of time the person appears in court, along with someone from the hospital, to have a judge decide if he or she needs continued hospitalization. By that time the patient usually has decided to sign in to the hospital voluntarily to avoid the court hassles.

As I said, adults more often find themselves in this position, for they can refuse to sign themselves in to the hospital for treatment. Let's assume that even though you are in the hospital on a voluntary status, you are still there *against your will.*

When you are hospitalized against your will, you will encounter locked doors. Sometimes they are meant to keep you locked inside; sometimes they are meant to keep others (more confused or dangerous) locked inside. Hospitals vary, so the examples I give here must be taken as such.

In most hospitals at least some of the wards are locked, or they are locked on the inside but open to anyone who wants to enter.

The unit will have some sort of seclusion room. Called "quiet rooms" or "time-out" rooms, they are used differently depending on the philosophy of the hospital. I have worked in places where the seclusion rooms were made of concrete and linoleum. They were stripped bare, not to provide a barren environment but a safe place where the person would not be able to hurt himself.

There is usually a window in the door so that the staff can monitor the patient.

For some people it is a living horror to be locked inside a small room, peered at by staff, and let out only at their discretion. For others the experience is comforting because the absence of stimulation allows them to settle down on their own. They can be away from the noise on the ward without danger to themselves. And to some who have lost touch with reality, it may not matter if they ever come out.

At another hospital where I worked, the walls and floor were carpeted so that a patient could flail about without risk of injury. Even when a person was thrashing around trying to hurt himself and everyone in his vicinity, the staff used their bodies to hold him until the outburst had subsided. The teenager was never left alone in the room. A staff member stayed with him, and the door was always left partly open.

Of course, the rooms can be used punitively. As I said, they are extensions of the staff's philosophy. If they believe patients should be cornered and controlled, that is what they will do.

On a locked ward you are sure to come into contact with violent, confused patients. A young woman I know was hospitalized for depression. Although she was not afraid of the other patients, who, she said, were constantly being dragged down the halls at night and put in the seclusion room, she was worried about getting in the middle of a scuffle between the staff and a patient.

Other teenagers have told me that they were frightened of their more aggressive peers and tried to keep their distance from them by following the staff members around.

In some hospitals you will encounter "levels of freedom." You start off on the ward with few if any freedoms; as you demonstrate more stability and trustworthiness—however that is decided—you gain more freedoms: the freedom to walk unescorted to meals, for instance, or to attend an activity off the locked ward. Even telephone privileges have to be earned at some facilities. One teenager remembers that as the most traumatic part of her hospitalization: the fear that she might do something the staff didn't like, and they would take away her telephone privileges.

You can be medicated against your will if your behavior presents a danger to anyone, including yourself. Of course, danger is in the eye of the beholder—the doctor. That can leave you in a pickle if you do not think you are "out of control." Medication is ideally used to combat the symptoms of your illness, whether those are confusion, depression, anxiety, or violence. You have the right not to get well, within reason. You can stay confused and disoriented as long as you are not hurting yourself or anyone else. Not eating and drinking because you are too confused to realize that you need to do so can be construed as suicidal behavior, and you can be medicated to lessen the confusion.

What happens if you run away from the hospital?

First of all, it depends on whether you are a voluntary admission or involuntarily committed. If you are not voluntary—or even if you are, but the staff considers you a danger to yourself or others—they are obligated to call the police to find you and bring you back.

Peggy, whom you will remember from the last chapter, ran away twice. The first time she ran off with Sharon, a patient who was involuntarily committed. The police found them at a boyfriend's house, and they took Sharon with them back to the hospital.

"Hey, what about me?" Peggy asked. "I ran away, too."

The policeman called the hospital to verify this and then said to Peggy, "You don't have to come back unless you want to."

"They don't want me?" she asked.

"You're not court-ordered there, so you're free to leave," he said.

"Well, I don't have anywhere else to go, so I might as well go back with Sharon."

The second time Peggy ran away—a month later—she did not go back.

Understand, too, that the staff has the right to go through your belongings within reason. They will invariably search your things when you first come to the unit. They may take away sharp things such as razors or nail files and clips, not necessarily because they think you might harm yourself with them but because someone else might get hold of them and use them. If you have an eating disorder or a drug problem, the staff may search you each time you leave the unit or have visitors to make sure you haven't acquired anything you shouldn't. It feels demeaning to have someone paw through your stuff; I hate it when the airport people go through my purse. But the airport personnel act for everyone's safety, and so does the nursing staff.

What will the staff expect of you? Most of all, they will want you to cooperate and participate. Probably some of the staff will want you to "get better," but you are not supposed to "get better" just to make the staff feel good. Ideally, the staff will realize that you will not get better overnight. If you are taking medication you may not see good results from it until after a week or longer.

Adolescence is a time for figuring out your place in society. You are not an adult, and you are not really a kid.

Your job is to grow wiser and stronger and away from your family, so that in a few years you can live on your own. Oddly enough, the adolescent has to reject his parents in some ways (or he thinks he has to) in order to achieve that independence. He bugs his parents and belittles them and makes them seem unimportant, so that when the time comes he can leave them and build his own life. Most authority figures receive the same treatment. The adolescent resists their efforts to mold him because he wants to do it on his own. All of that is *normal* adolescence. It is doubly hard for the adolescent who is also dealing with an emotional disorder. He has to contend not only with the normal rejecting period of adolescence but also the uncomfortable, frightening, out-of-control symptoms of his illness. The competent staff will be sensitive to the adolescent and anticipate his occasional resistance and stubborn lack of improvement.

All staff must maintain proper boundaries. That means they will not initiate sex with you nor accept your sexual advances. The staff do not have the right to abuse you physically, verbally, or sexually. Likewise, you do not have the right to abuse them, even if your judgment is badly compromised right now. If you do try to hurt someone, even the most understanding staff member will try to stop you. That does not mean hurting you back; legally they can only take measures to stop the attack.

Above all else, you have the right to be treated with dignity and respect, and that includes not being talked down to. When I was a hospital aide years ago I got a glimpse of what that meant. The rule that nurses and aides had to wear white clothes had just been lifted, and we were all decked out in street clothes. I was coming down the hallway after supervising lunch in the cafeteria when a new doctor approached me. I smiled and said, "Hello."

"How are you?" the doctor said, and then, "Are you on your way back to your ward?"

Just the sappy tone of his voice—that mixture of condescension and coercion—made me realize that he thought I was a patient. I felt humiliated for all the patients who had to hear that tone in any of our voices—as if we were better than they.

While I was working as an aide at that hospital, I was also working on my Master's Degree in Human Relations. My particular graduate program must have drawn all the idealistic, discontented students in the country, and there we sat each week trying to come to grips with a world not to our liking. Specifically, there was I writing idealistic papers against traditional mental institutions and working right in the thick of things in the evenings. One day I had just finished a paper about the dignity of the mentally ill patient when a free-for-all broke out on the unit. A pregnant teenager who was as mean-spirited as she was confused was throwing chairs and generally trying to tear up the place. I called for male assistance and joined the other female aide already trying to contain the girl. Carefully we wrestled her into the seclusion room. We stood there with our arms wrapped around her because we couldn't figure out how to get out of the room without knocking her down and hurting her.

And there I was, thinking that I should still treat this girl (who was obviously out of control) with dignity and compassion. She looked up at me just then, smiled, and said, "Carolyn, as soon as those male aides get here I'm going to rip your dress off. You just watch."

Although there is no excuse for not holding onto your ideals, let me say that sometimes it takes a major effort.

Supposedly only good things will happen to you in the

hospital (you'll find a therapist you can trust and relief for your symptoms), but the truth is that bad things *do* happen to good people. Some staff members may treat you discourteously; some may even treat you inhumanely. Why could that happen? Well, all of us have bad days and times when our own problems overwhelm us. Sometimes the staff person will be preoccupied with her own problems, and it makes her far less responsive to you. Understand, I am not excusing her behavior; I'm saying that she may act "better" on some days than on others. Realize, too, that not only qualified people are drawn to this profession. Sometimes people are drawn to it for the wrong reasons. Most staff members are underpaid and overworked, and they may have taken this job because it was the first one for which they applied.

People who do not like or understand adolescents in the first place have trouble with their own issues of control and power because those are the very issues the adolescents have trouble with: *control* (over their out-of-control body), *power* (because they do not seem to have any), and *autonomy* (which is the ability—or need, in their case—to do things on their own).

What can you do if you think the staff is not treating you fairly? Is there anything you can do short of running away?

If I were in a hospital, I would first find an ally, preferably a powerful ally. A patient for a friend is fine, but he is as helpless as you in confronting the staff. I would put my trust in my therapist (unless he were the one mistreating me) and ask him to help me smooth things over. If my therapist were not effective in intervening in my behalf, I would talk to my parents or perhaps a lawyer.

Don't call the local television station and complain about the way the hospital is run. For one thing, that is likely to ruffle more feathers than it smooths. Furthermore, the television staff is not likely to believe what you say if you present it hysterically. They'll mark you off as a confused mental patient.

I cannot stress enough that *you need someone on your side*. It is best if that is done from within the building, although a well-informed, assertive family member can be a godsend.

Be sure, however, that your illness has not clouded your thinking so that you don't realize that you haven't got a case. In other words, be sure you are not truly paranoid, thinking that everyone is out to get you. Sometimes part of your illness may be not seeing the world accurately. People may be treating you better than you think, or they may be responding to your own provocative behavior.

You can always ask to leave the hospital. If you are under eighteen you need a guardian or parent to come to get you; and if you are considered still at risk (whether you think so or not), the doctors can sign papers to make you stay, at least until a court decides your case.

Being anywhere under lock and key is unnerving, but bad things do not have to happen while you are hospitalized. Remember, it *is* temporary. You will get out eventually, although hospitalization for teenagers can run into months. You have to trust that the doctors, therapists, and nursing staff have your best interests at heart. If you do not believe that, you must muster the energy to do something about it.

It is easy to think that the "little person" always gets the worst of it, but a well-informed "little person" carries a lot of clout. Don't lose sight of that.

CHAPTER ◇ 10

Making the Best of It

When an adolescent is hospitalized, usually his family has explored all the less restrictive ways of treating his problem. Hospitalization, then, is really for those with the most serious symptoms of emotional disorder. As a rule, those who fare the best are the ones with the best support system and compensating strengths.

How is the adolescent supposed to get better? Or put more simply, how do the symptoms go away?

First of all, there is such a thing as "spontaneous recovery." In rare cases the person gets better for no apparent reason.

When I was a social worker I was assigned to work on a ward where none of the patients were getting better. It was not the choicest ward, as you can imagine, because the social worker rarely got to see anyone improve. The work was routine and unrewarding, but I had a few favorite patients I liked to keep track of. One of those patients was a woman of my mother's age named Tess.

I had first met Tess in 1973 when I came to the hospital as an aide and knew nothing about mentally ill people. Tess had wandered into the nurse's station when all the other staff members were somewhere else, and I was at a loss as to how to get her out. I followed her around as she poured herself a cup of coffee, and she kept shouting at me the filthiest words I had ever heard. Finally another nurse came back to the ward and said, "Tess, you know you're not supposed to be in here. Go on out to the dayroom."

And Tess wandered out, still cursing me and the weather and the whole state.

"Weren't you afraid of her?" I asked the nurse.

"Of Tess?" she said, laughing. "Tess wouldn't hurt a fly."

"But she threatened me," I said.

"Oh, she always talks like that."

"What's she in here for?" I asked. I was sure it had to be murder.

"She's just crazy. She used to be a teacher. That's what's so funny about her dirty language. Can you imagine a schoolteacher talking like that?"

That was my introduction to schizophrenia. Tess had been diagnosed as having chronic schizophrenia and had little hope of getting better. Perhaps it was because I had always wanted to be a teacher, or maybe it was because Tess was my mother's age, and she came from New England, as I had. In any event, I grew fond of Tess and was glad to find her years later as one of my patients on the ward.

In 1978, five years after she had been admitted, Tess fell and broke her hip. She was transferred to the medical part of the psychiatric hospital where her hip could be surgically repaired. For five years her husband had faithfully visited her each week and provided spending money for her. However, he had become convinced that she would not get better. In all that time, no amount of medicine had cleared up her thinking; she was locked in her own private world where she spewed insults to imaginary people she believed were torturing her. No amount of therapy or activities had made any impression on her. So her husband obtained a divorce and remarried. Their schizophrenic daughter apparently did well on the outside as long as she had no contact with her mother.

I continued to visit Tess on the medical unit, and I maintained contact with her family despite the divorce. Although Tess could only recognize me as "Little Miss Sunshine—you despicable witch," I still wanted to spend time with her. Maybe out of guilt; I would not have wanted my own mother to be abandoned like that.

Imagine my shock one morning when I went to visit Tess and found her sitting up in bed reading a book. Not a magazine: a book!

She looked puzzled when she saw me. "Are you a new nurse?" she asked. "I don't know you."

"I'm Little Miss Sunshine—the despicable witch, don't you remember?" I asked.

"No, I'm sorry, I don't remember you. Did I call you that?"

Her politeness threw me off balance. This was not the Tess I knew.

"How are you feeling?" I asked because I couldn't think of anything more profound to say.

"Well, I'm not sure. Where am I supposed to be?"

"Don't you remember being admitted to the hospital?"

"Vaguely," she said. "How many days have I been here?"

"Days?" I cried. "You've been hospitalized five years."

"Five years?" Tess said. "Where is John? Who's watching our daughter?"

"John?" I asked, and I felt guilty merely knowing that he had divorced her.

"Doesn't he still visit me?"

"Of course, he does. But Tess, we never realized you were going to get better," I said.

None of the doctors could explain why Tess had gotten better. She had been taking the same medicine for years, with periodic changes that were unsuccessful at managing her symptoms. She had been involved in all the therapies, and many social workers had spent hours with her and her family. The only thing different was her fall and the subsequent surgery. Overnight she had returned to being Tess, the former schoolteacher. The voices were gone, and her filthy language was a thing of the past.

Tess continued to improve physically and emotionally. In 1979 I accompanied her by plane back to Boston where she was reunited with her sister. In all that time, and in the subsequent letters she wrote me, she suffered no recurrence of symptoms. For some unexplained reason, she had experienced a spontaneous recovery.

Granted, Tess's experience was remarkable. Most often you will see improvement only after taking medicine, for example. Specific medications are geared toward eradicating specific symptoms, but sometimes you have to weigh the benefits against the side effects. Unpleasant but tolerable side effects include dry mouth, blurred vision, and temporarily diminished sexual response. Less tolerable side effects include akathesia, in which your body seems to have an extreme case of the jitters (You want to stand up and sit down at the same time), and a dystonic reaction, which is a frightening involuntary drawing up of your facial and neck muscles. These symptoms can be diminished with "side effect medicine" called anticholinergics, which are given along with the regular medicine to reduce the severity of the side effects. Unfortunately, people who fool around with these potent drugs have discovered that too much of a good thing can induce psychotic symptoms: disorientation and hallucinations. Let your doctor decide when and how much of these types of medications you need.

Antidepressants take longer to "work" than the major tranquilizers or antianxiety medications. With the tricyclic antidepressants you may have to wait two weeks for the drug to build up to the proper level in your bloodstream. With a major tranquilizer, you should see the sedative effects almost immediately. If the medication is going to work, remission (disappearance) of symptoms (the foggy thinking, the "voice commands") occurs within a week, if not sooner. No reputable doctor will release a person on a dose of medicine that keeps him only half awake. Instead, the doctor tries to decrease the dosage to an acceptable but still functional level, which may prolong the hospital stay until the doctor knows that the lower dosage works.

Sometimes a person gets better just by being in a structured environment. Augusta, a pregnant teenager admitted to the hospital for severe depression, could not be medicated without risk to the fetus. The staff tried a different treatment with her. They altered her sleeping pattern to see if her symptoms would diminish with the rearranged hours. They also had her sit under a sunlamp for phototherapy sessions in the hope that her depression would respond to the increased time in the sunlight. Augusta did improve, whether because her illness had run its course or because she responded to the phototherapy.

Sometimes a person's getting better hinges on how well he makes use of the hospital services offered. Does he attend therapy groups, and if so does he talk or sit back counting the minutes until the session is over? Group therapy is a powerful treatment for the adolescent. (Some hospitals divide patients into two groups, one for the more verbal patients, and the other for those with shortened attention spans.) Teenagers may dislike these groups for the very reason that they are so effective. Kids cannot hide from other kids. Adults may misread some adolescents, but other adolescents do not. In a group I conducted at the hospital, a girl who had a long history of sexual abuse gently confronted another girl with no reported history of abuse. Martha asked the second girl point-blank *when* she had been abused. Of course, the second girl denied being abused.

"Well, I'm not going to make you talk about it," Martha said. "But I've been abused myself and I know a victim when I see one. You, I'm afraid, show all the signs."

It was not until a week later that Dorian (the girl from an earlier chapter whose older sister had died of leukemia) admitted that she had been abused as a child by her idealized sister. What she had been keeping secret, and part of the reason she had so much trouble mourning her sister's death, had been uncovered by another patient who had gone through a similar experience.

At many hospitals you will undergo a whole battery of tests to determine your strengths and deficits, your overall coping style and brain function. Not all hospitals administer every test mentioned here, and some may not do any testing. To familiarize you with some of the procedures, I asked my friend and former colleague Dr. Greg Carbone, Director of Psychological Testing Services at Jackson Brook Institute, to comment on the tests he typically uses and the reasons he relies on them.

To assess the teenager's cognitive functioning (how the

person thinks), Dr. Carbone uses a test that is essentially a series of questions and games designed to test the person's concentration and attention, how well he can figure out situations (social situations as well as puzzles), and how fast he can process (understand) information. If you took this test, you would be asked to look at a series of pictures to determine what was missing; you would be asked questions about what you might do in certain social situations; and you would be asked questions to demonstrate how much you know about general kinds of things. The best part about this test is that you can't flunk it.

Dr. Carbone also does educational testing with some teenagers. Achievement tests measure performance in reading and spelling and reveal any learning disabilities. For instance, if a person has an average IQ but is not performing up to expectations in school, he may have a reading disability that prevents him from grasping the information he reads. Most people try to hide deficiencies (by rowdy behavior, being the class clown) because they perceive them as weaknesses, something to be ashamed of. The purpose of testing, however, is to determine what the problem areas are and to identify the strengths that can compensate for the weaknesses. Even if someone is less than adept in a certain area, he or she usually has some other area in which he is good. The psychologist looks for the good points so that the therapist can help the adolescent capitalize on those strengths.

Dr. Carbone sometimes uses personality tests to confirm information that the therapist already suspects. The Minnesota Multiphasic Personality Inventory (MMPI) is a set of five hundred questions that you answer on your own. You are asked to report on your feelings and behavior. The test is designed to give the psychologist a picture of how you cope with life. It can indicate whether you are suffering from a thought disorder or an emotional disturbance, or both, and what type of emotional disturbance: depression, a conduct disorder, and so on.

Other personality tests are called "projective tests" because they involve the person's making up stories about pictures presented. You might be asked to draw-a-person, or to do a kinetic family drawing. With the thematic apperception test (TAT), you are asked to tell a story about each of the pictures presented. With the famous inkblot test, you are shown a series of inkblots and asked what they remind you of. There are no right or wrong answers. You simply describe what you see or what comes to mind, which reveals to the psychologist what your mind is on, what the turmoil is.

Finally, there are neuropsychological tests that document brain functioning. CAT scans are sometimes used to detect gross abnormalities in the brain, a tumor, for instance, that might account for recent behavioral change. EEGs are done to rule out a seizure disorder. Both tests are painless, though they look scary because of all the machines and wires. If you know you are scheduled to have any test, ask your doctor specifically why you're being given the test, what the doctors are looking for, and what the experience will be like. You have a right to this information. You also have a right to refuse to take the tests, though in that case the staff may claim that you are refusing treatment. I think you'll find that most of the tests, though time-consuming, are fun to take. At least more fun than sitting through doctor's rounds.

Speaking of doctor's rounds, you will probably be seeing the doctor three times a week or more so he can judge your situation, specifically how you are doing and whether or not you still need hospitalization. Do not expect to meet with the doctor one-to-one for more than a few minutes;

there is not enough time in the day to do that with all his patients. But if you leave notes detailing your questions or requests, the doctor should get back with you within the day.

When a person is first admitted to an accredited hospital, the primary therapist and doctor make up a treatment plan that sets out the course of treatment and the projected discharge date. See? *You will get out*. You have a right to know just when the staff thinks you will be ready to leave the hospital. But don't be surprised if your projected discharge date mysteriously coincides with the date your insurance expires.

You should receive a lot of attention in the hospital from a battery of people who are working toward getting you well: talk therapy groups, occupational and recreational therapy groups, nutrition groups, doctor's rounds, and family meetings. What you will not have at most places (there are always exceptions) is time on your hands. I once had a patient who asked to leave the hospital because she "came here to relax, not go to all these groups." The truth is that you are not in a psychiatric hospital to get some rest. You go to a spa for that.

Once you know you are on the mend and will be released soon, you may have second thoughts. Am I really well enough to handle the stresses out there? Will I make a fool of myself in public? How do I know if my control is back? What will people say when they see me?

Of course, I cannot tell you the answers to those questions. You probably can't answer them yourself, nor can your therapists and doctors, which is why they will no doubt send you home on trial visits before discharging you. You prepare for your eventual discharge by going home on short passes—either overnight or daytime visits—to assess how things go. Naturally you will feel awkward with all that freedom back and all those people around you. They will feel awkward, too, because they will not know how you will act or how *they* should act. You might as well confront the awkwardness and get it in the open. Don't pretend that everything is as it was. Chances are you will relax once you admit your discomfort. Remember, if things get difficult you can always go back to the hospital early.

A word about labeling. We live in an intolerant, often unkind society. Some people will think you are *dangerous* because you have been hospitalized. The ones who will fear you the most are probably the very ones who fear for their own emotional control. That is the bad part about a psychiatrie diagnosis: Some people will use the label to brand you because whatever is different with you is something they don't understand. You cannot change society, but you can change individuals one at a time. Don't think you have to tolerate anyone's treating you badly; speak out. It is the best way to show that you have not lost your mind. And hang onto your sense of humor; it helps keep things in perspective.

CHAPTER ◇ 11

How Did You Become Ill in the First Place?

To appreciate this chapter, you should realize that in previous times "sick" people were always blamed for their illness. (Even today, people often believe that "you get what you deserve.") If the illness was not God punishing you for some imagined sin you had committed, it was the devil who had taken over your body and mind.

In more recent times society has blamed "the mother" for everything from her children's poor academic performance to their behavioral outbursts in public. (I used to believe everything was my mother's fault, too, until *I* became a mother!) Now that two parents are sharing childrearing, society is handing the father part of the blame for "ruining" the child.

But scientists and sociologists are having second thoughts. Maybe it is not all Mom's fault after all, and maybe it isn't the kid's either. Now sociologists are beginning to understand the combination of forces that come into play to create the environment for an emotional disorder. Theorists speculate that some people have a biological vulnerability to certain emotional disorders, just as others do to heart disease if it runs in the family. Not all people have the emotional strength to manage that stress in their lives, and they succumb more readily to emotional problems.

Despite their biological sensitivity toward illness, other people may manage quite well, never experiencing symptoms of depression or mania because the stress level in their lives is minimal. It is usually when the two factors, biological and social, come together that people have trouble. Then they are unable to separate out which caused the problems in the first place.

Scientists speculate, too, that specific genes may make a person more likely to develop substance-abuse problems or depression. If that is the case, of how much use would it be to "will" yourself to overcome this weakness and of what use is it to berate yourself for having it? Better to accept that scientists cannot yet isolate and control which genes you acquire from your parents or which illnesses you may have a tendency to contract. Accept, too, that if you arrange your life so that stress is more manageable, you may not get the particular disorder or you may be able to minimize its effects.

For example, if your family has a history of heart disease and your father died recently of a heart attack, you probably know that you are at risk for developing heart disease. That is not to say that you will get the disease. But if you work toward decreasing the risk (by exercising, following a sensible diet, minimizing work and family stress), you may never get it. Your biological history may *predispose* you toward the disease, but everything else that happens in your life can affect whether you end up with it or not.

Why do some people get depressed while others do not, even though they all seem to be in the same circumstances?

Because not all people are in the same circumstances.

People differ in their physical health, their financial state, their support systems, and their ability to bounce back from adversity. When I first started working at Jackson Brook Institute, Dr. Rollin Ives (who has since gone on to be the State Commissioner of Human Services) was the clinical director of the hospital. He continually drilled into us the importance of identifying the patient's *strengths*, not just his vulnerabilities. In that way we could tell the patient, "The bad news is that you don't have the stability (or whatever) to do *this*, but the good news is that you can do these other things."

"It is simply not true that some people can be anything they want to be if they just put their mind to it," Dr. Ives said to me on more than one occasion.

For people with multiple physical problems and learning disabilities, for example, it may be that they cannot do everything that their healthier neighbor can, but there may be other ways of accomplishing their goals.

Let's compare two hypothetical people. One has had diabetes since childhood, necessitating several hospitalizations. He has missed a lot of school, and he doesn't have many friends. His mother works two jobs to support the family because his father is fired from all of his jobs for drinking. Two of his uncles have been treated for depression, and a distant cousin committed suicide.

The other person comes from a stable family background, with both parents in the home. He is healthy and of average intelligence. There is no known history of emotional disorders in the family.

Which person do you think has the better chance of combatting the added stress of a death in the family? Which one do you think has the strength to tolerate such an event? Obviously the second person seems to have less "wrong" in his life. The first person is troubled not only by physical illness but severe family stress, school difficulties, and other emotional illness at home. The cards seem stacked against him.

And if this person fell into a severe depression that required hospitalization, would it be because someone had died? Or would it be a combination of factors culminating in the last straw—a loved one's death?

A story that Dr. Ives often told was about a young boy with a reading difficulty that kept him from easily understanding what he read, no matter how many times he read it. At first others thought this boy was "slow" because he struggled so hard to get average grades. But when he underwent tests it was discovered that he had a learning disability: a weakness in processing (understanding) written material. The boy found out, however, that if he read *out loud* he could more easily understand and remember. And so he got through high school and went on to college. Although it was not fun for him to read books, he managed to compensate for his problem enough to get on with his life.

Was this a story Dr. Ives made up to inspire us? No. It is *his own* story, and the ending is that now he is a state commissoner, responsible for thousands of people's well-being.

Sometimes there are specific reasons for developing an emotional disorder. Fooling arour with drugs is a way to bring on something that is beyond your power to control. Many clinicians believe that people who abuse drugs or alcohol do so to try to medicate their pain themselves, dulling their depression or trying to lighten their mood. Of course, street drugs and alcohol will not do either. Often, in fact, they contribute to more aggressive behavior, in no way solving your original problem.

Steroids have been found to cause psychotic symptoms in some people. Some prescription drugs taken in combination with others produce psychotic symptoms, which is why you should always tell your doctor *all* the medicines you are taking.

Brain injuries can cause disturbed behavior, and unfortunately they are permanent. Medication may lessen the symptoms of agitation, but it will not restore the person to his or her original capacities.

Nutritional deficiencies can cause behavioral disturbances, which may make it hard to decide which comes first, the eating disorder or the emotional disturbance.

As mentioned in an earlier chapter, "crazy" situations at home can cause a person to develop an emotional disorder. An example is the abuse victim, who suffers not only assaults to his or her dignity but the shame of being helpless. Feeling guilty that the situation is somehow his fault or perhaps angry that no one will respond to his pleas, the victim develops depression or other behavioral disturbances.

In sum, it would be simpler if you could blame a specific person or a specific event for causing an emotional disorder. But there is rarely one single cause. Think of the teenagers you have known who have been abused or have done poorly in school. Did they all develop an emotional disorder that required professional treatment? Or do you suppose that for some kids additional circumstances pushed them over the edge?

CHAPTER ◇ 12

The Road Back to Health

With treatment and support, most of you will bounce back from an emotional disorder. But to stay well, you will have to make some changes in your life.

Those of you who are medicated need to take the medicine even after you leave the hospital. If you have ever had an infection treated with an antibiotic, you know that you have to take the whole supply of medicine even if the symptoms disappear after a few days. Likewise with emotional problems, *you have to keep on taking the medicine* even if the symptoms have gone away. Usually, the symptoms disappear *because* you are taking the medicine. If you suddenly stopped taking it, not only would you be likely to redevelop the symptoms, but you could induce seizures and other complications.

Some people believe that a drug abuser should not be medicated at all. Some doctors say that depends on why you were abusing the drug or alcohol in the first place. If you have an underlying depression, you may have unwittingly been treating the pain with your own remedy. Your body may actually need a chemical to alter an imbalance, although street drugs and alcohol are not the treatments of choice. If the substance you were abusing were simply removed, you would still be left with your depression and the chemical imbalance. Doctors prescribe medication in those cases to correct the imbalance without risking further addiction. You do not develop drug dependence on antidepressants.

You may not have to take medicine the rest of your life. Doctors are reluctant to start teenagers on medication in the first place, and most doctors do not intend for the teenager to take pills for years. But trust your doctor to decide—*with your input*—when you are well enough to stop taking the medicine.

If you are involved in family therapy sessions, do not expect your problems to fade without more problems arising in the family itself. Inevitably, when one person has been identified with "the problem" for a long time, it is hard for the other members to give up that scapegoat. The adolescent's starting to get better might mean more disharmony among the other family members. But keep at it. Family therapy is hard work. Before everyone gets better they may experience new problems and renewed anger, because even unhappy families grow accustomed to the way things have been and do not want to change.

It's one thing to make friends with the other patients on the ward; it's quite another to assume all of their problems. Much as you may think you can help in their struggles, leave the job to the professionals. Your task is to get yourself well and move on.

A lot of patients bond with other patients in the same

circumstances. You may develop strong ties with your peers out of the sense of "we-ness" on the ward. (You know, "us" against "them"—the staff, the families.) But the "we-ness" fades after you've left the ward, unless the two or three of you have more in common than your problems and your hospital address. It doesn't mean you've deserted each other; it simply means you've gone on, and that's as it should be.

By now, when you are ready for discharge, you will have looked at both your vulnerabilities and your strengths. Some vulnerabilities cannot be changed, including your intellectual capacities. If your therapist has done his or her job, however, he will have explained that your weak areas do not make you any less of a person. Everyone has his own weak spots. What you have to do is rely on your other abilities to cover for those weak areas. Sometimes you become depressed all over again because you expect (unrealistically) either to return to "normal" or to be able to do things you don't have the ability to do. We cannot be all things.

Once you are back out in the world, think about your friendships. Are your friends supportive of you, or do they treat you with kid gloves because they think you may get "sick" again? Do they sabotage your efforts to get well? For example, do they encourage you to follow doctor's orders or do they want to see you back the way you used to be: doing drugs, drinking, engaging in risky behavior? If so, you need to wonder about their motives. You may have to find a whole new circle of friends if your old friends reinforce the dangerous way you were living.

Granted, it will take an effort to start over, but the better your support system, the better your chances for a full and lasting recovery. Joining a mental health support group will introduce you to others in similar circumstances and also give you a place to go with questions about "life after treatment." Your community counseling service or mental health center can direct you to such groups.

After all your work with a therapist, you may find that your problems lessen if you change your circumstances at home. You may decide to leave home (if you are old enough or mature enough) or switch the parent you live with. If you are already living on your own, you may decide to return to your family. You may decide not to shoulder so many burdens, dropping an extra job or delaying college. Perhaps you will want to change courses in high school or find an alternative to going to regular classes. There are dozens of alternatives you can explore to lessen the stress you have encountered in the past. All it calls for is flexibility on your part, a willingness to make the needed changes.

One of my former high school students is now in her mid-twenties. In high school Carla got sidetracked by her problems at home and her hard-drinking friends. And like her friends, she dropped out of school. Following therapy she felt better about herself and was able to make some healthy changes in her life. She got a job that "made me have to be responsible." Later she married and started a family. Then, several years later, she returned to school to get her diploma. Carla was always an above-average student, but her stress at home and the teacher's inability to reach out to her prevented her from doing well. Now she has graduated and is more certain of the positive direction she wants her life to take. She accomplished her original goals only after reordering her priorities.

Your outpatient therapist will be a large part of your support system after you leave the hospital. He or she will be there with you as you try out new circumstances and "positive addictions"—hobbies or sports. Getting out of the hospital does not mean that you no longer have problems to work on.

In recommending outpatient therapy to a friend recently, Dwain explained, "If you were a baseball pitcher, and one day you discovered that you were not pitching the same type of game anymore—that something was wrong—what would happen?"

The friend responded, "Well, the coach would probably have someone watch me throw for a while to see why my game was off."

"Exactly," Dwain said. "When your pitch is off—when something is wrong—you have another person watch your game to point out what you're doing differently. That's what a good therapist does; he sits back and watches your game."

But there comes a time when you want to end your sessions because you are strong enough not to need them anymore. Therapy sessions are supposed to end when you have accomplished what you *realistically* wanted from them.

When I was an outpatient therapist I saw a young girl for a number of years. Just when I thought she was doing well on her own, and we started to consider terminating the sessions, Diane began to get depressed and agitated.

"I guess I'm just a mess," she told me.

"What's that supposed to mean?" I asked.

"Well, I'm still depressed, and I keep having these bad thoughts," she said.

"Bad thoughts about what?"

"That I'm not really well enough to be on my own."

"Do *you* think you're well enough?" I asked.

"I don't know," she said.

"Sometimes you have to try it to see," I said. "I think you're strong enough."

"But what if something goes wrong? Can I get back in to see you? Or will you give away my appointment time?" she asked.

"Well, Diane," I said, "I'm going to give your time slot to someone else because I think you're going to do just fine. But I'll always make room to see you again if you want to come in."

"You probably won't want to see me if I'm not sick, right?" she asked.

"Of course not," I said. "You can call me just to tell me you're doing okay. You don't have to be having a problem first."

"You'd want to see me every now and then?" she asked.

"I will still be here for you, no matter what," I said. And that was the issue.

Diane's symptoms cleared up by the next session. She was able to say good-bye to me after she realized that her flare-up of symptoms sprang from her fear that she had to be "sick" to keep me as a support.

You are going to get well, believe that. And when you do, you will be ready to say good-bye to those who have helped you along. Just as adolescence sparks feelings of desire and regret about leaving your parents, so too leaving your therapist may trigger feelings of loss. Sometimes it is just plain hard to give up the familiarity of your problems and talking about them once a week. Getting on with your life—going forward—always means leaving certain things behind. And certain people.

When Dwain was terminating with a young boy, in the last few sessions the boy brought up his anger at his mother who had given him up for adoption. As he stormed against this woman he hardly knew, it occurred to Dwain that the boy (who had not talked much about his mother in the past) was telling Dwain that he was angry and sad about leaving him too.

The boy was not just reinventing old symptoms to prolong his therapy. He was moving out of state and knew he had to end treatment with Dwain. But he was overwhelmed by feelings of loss that brought back all his previous losses. Once Dwain saw that his client was grieving all those losses, he could help the boy say good-bye to him as well.

CHAPTER ◇ 13

Will It Happen Again?

If you have ever experienced an emotional disorder, particularly if you have been hospitalized for one, you probably worry that your symptoms will return. Let's look at your prognosis for the future, the chances for your continued well-being.

How long you remain symptom-free depends on many things. Factors may never combine in such a way as to produce a relapse. But the prognosis for some disorders is better than for others. For example, schizophrenia is more difficult to treat than depression or other mood disorders. You might continue to take medicine for years and still have a recurrence of symptoms. Sometimes a medication for obsessive compulsive disorder stops being effective, and the old routines and repetitive thoughts return. Thus, although you may be recovered, you may be like the person with diabetes—always in need of monitoring.

Staying well also depends on following doctor's orders. If there are specific plans for your continued recovery after leaving the hospital, follow them to the best of your ability. It is usually when someone decides he has nothing further to be concerned about that he relapses.

Need I mention that a positive attitude about your situation is better than a negative one? We often create the very circumstances we constantly have on our mind. If you keep dreading that something bad will happen, you may end up with the very scenario you dread. You know that the paranoid person thinks everyone is trying to ruin his life. How is it that all the stuff he thinks people are doing to him usually comes true? Can it be that this is the reality he has constructed for himself?

Ally yourself with a therapist whom you like and trust. Do not continue with a therapist that everyone else thinks is great if you don't like him or her yourself. In the end you would have to withhold so much of yourself that the sessions would be unproductive. You do not have to stay with the first therapist you meet. Sometimes the alliance just does not work. Better to find someone you can relate to.

Join a support group (for abuse victims, former mental patients or alcoholics, etc.) so that you have a circle of friends to encourage you on your road to recovery.

Remember two other things. Even without a "cure" at the moment for your particular disorder, there is always hope for progress in that direction. Scientists are working to find the "miracle drug" that will cure certain disorders and also isolate the circumstances that might worsen a person's condition. At the same time, spiritualists are showing us ways to help heal ourselves. There is always that kind of HOPE.

Likewise, there's the hope that society will better understand those who have emotional disorders, and will treat them with dignity, not fear. Accorded more dignity, the person may behave with more dignity. Remember, *you have not gotten what you deserved*. If you have gotten better, it is not because God liked you better than He did another person on the ward. You have merely responded better to the treatment available. Have compassion for your friend who has not gotten better, and remember, *it is not his fault*. Society is unkind and unforgiving in general, but we are part of that society, and we can help people change.

Rachel was suffering from a bi-polar disorder in 1973 when I first worked with her. She couldn't slow down her thoughts or keep a lid on her energy. She wore us all out, as she tore around the ward. Rachel was close to my own age at the time, and I secretly felt sorry for her because her life was such a mess. Unless she took Lithium the rest of her life (or a large part of it), she wasn't going to be able to have a career or make something of herself. I was embarrassed for her because although it might be fun to be out-of-control once in awhile, it actually is scary never to be able to regain control of yourself.

Imagine my shock seven years later when I received a phone call from a welfare social worker about one of my clients. It was Rachel. Not the client—but the welfare social worker. Rachel had indeed calmed down on Lithium and gotten her life back in order. Then she's gone on to college to work on a degree in social work. She was symptom-free, but more than that, she was happy. Married to a nice, young man who also had a career he was proud of.

When Rachel realized who *I* was—that I'd worked with her years earlier on the other ward—she said, "You know, I sometimes tell my welfare clients how easy it is to get the treatment they need. Afterall, I was once bouncing off the walls myself. When they realize, I'm okay now, they aren't so afraid of taking that first step."

"I can't believe you're doing so well," I said.

"Didn't you think I'd ever get well?" she asked.

"Well, I hoped," I said, unconvincingly.

"I *believed*," she said. "And *that* must have made the difference."

CHAPTER ◇ 14

Symptoms Checklist and Steps for Getting Treatment

Check off any symptoms you have been experiencing, but remember *it is up to the therapist to draw a conclusion*. Many of these symptoms, viewed separately, are normal reactions. It is only in the larger picture that they mean something.

MOOD

- ☐ 1. Periods of being down.
- ☐ 2. Hopelessness, listlessness.
- ☐ 3. Lack of energy.
- ☐ 4. Apathy, not caring about anything.
- ☐ 5. Loss of interest in things that used to give you pleasure.
- ☐ 6. Periods of high energy and excitability.

- ☐ 7. Extreme fluctuations in mood.
- ☐ 8. Feeling that life isn't worth living.
- ☐ 9. Specific plans for suicide.
- ☐ 10. Desire to be dead, but no plan.
- ☐ 11. Periods of dread and fear.

YOUR THINKING

- ☐ 1. Thoughts racing uncontrollably.
- ☐ 2. One repetitive thought interferes with your ability to carry on with your life.
- ☐ 3. Voices heard either in your head or outside it that tell you what to do or simply taunt you.
- ☐ 4. Inability to concentrate or make decisions.
- ☐ 5. People telling you that your perceptions of things are not accurate.
- ☐ 6. Belief that people are talking behind your back or want to harm you.
- ☐ 7. Desire to spend more money than you have or to enter into shady schemes.
- ☐ 8. Difficulty understanding what is expected of you.
- ☐ 9. Fear that you could not contain behaviors if you started engaging in them.
- ☐ 10. Preoccupation with thoughts.
- ☐ 11. Belief that you are evil.
- ☐ 12. Belief that everything is either black or white, good or bad.

CHANGES IN BEHAVIOR

- ☐ 1. Difficulty in understanding school assignments.
- ☐ 2. Inability to do schoolwork or hold a job.
- ☐ 3. Getting into trouble with authority figures (teachers, police, parents).

- ☐ 4. Having to perform certain rituals over and over.
- ☐ 5. Sleep disturance (sleeping either more or less).
- ☐ 6. Early morning awakening.
- ☐ 7. Change in appetite (weight gain or loss).
- ☐ 8. Withdrawing from people.
- ☐ 9. Vomiting after meals.
- ☐ 10. Alternating extreme dieting with eating binges.
- ☐ 11. Sometimes being rude or doing inappropriate things.
- ☐ 12. Spending more money.
- ☐ 13. Sexual promiscuity.
- ☐ 14. Loss of interest in sex or relationships.
- ☐ 15. Increased substance use.
- ☐ 16. Decreased substance use or abstinence.
- ☐ 17. Inability to stop doing certain things.
- ☐ 18. Racing, pounding heart.
- ☐ 19. The shakes.
- ☐ 20. Pain in the breastbone or around the heart.
- ☐ 21. Tingling arms.
- ☐ 22. Tingling face.
- ☐ 23. Blackouts, dizziness, light-headedness.
- ☐ 24. Headaches.
- ☐ 25. Diarrhea.
- ☐ 26. Constipation.
- ☐ 27. Stomachaches.
- ☐ 28. Inability to keep food down

SUBSTANCE USE

- ☐ 1. Abstinence.
- ☐ 2. Moderate use of
  alcohol
  marijuana.
  hallucinogens.

cocaine.
heroin.

3. Heavy use of:
alcohol.
marijuana.
hallucinogens.
cocaine.
heroin.

FAMILY HISTORY

☐ 1. Emotional problems in family members, whether treated or not.
☐ 2. Suicide attempts or actual suicides by family members.
☐ 3. Have you ever attempted suicide?
☐ 4. Have you ever considered suicide?
☐ 5. History of abuse (physical or sexual).
☐ 6. Family history of serious medical problems.
☐ 7. Family history of substance abuse or eating disorders.

CHANGES IN LIFE CIRCUMSTANCES

Check all changes that you have experienced in the last year.

☐ 1. Death in family.
☐ 2. Death of a peer.
☐ 3. Divorce in family.
☐ 4. Romantic breakup.
☐ 5. Beginning of a new relationship.
☐ 6. Discovery of own adoption.
☐ 7. Having sex for the first time.
☐ 8. An unplanned pregnancy.

- [ ] 9. Birth of a new sibling.
- [ ] 10. Moving.
- [ ] 11. Friend or family member moving away.
- [ ] 12. Hospitalization of a close family member or friend.
- [ ] 13. Failure to make a team, win an event.
- [ ] 14. Parent losing a job.
- [ ] 15. Sexual abuse, physical abuse.
- [ ] 16. Family financial problems.
- [ ] 17. Legal problems in family.
- [ ] 18. Physical illness (with or without hospitalization).
- [ ] 19. Losing your job.
- [ ] 20. House destroyed by fire.
- [ ] 21. Flunking a test or a course.

STEPS FOR GETTING TREATMENT

1. Make a symptoms inventory (using preceding checklist).
2. Contact:
    a. family physician, or
    b. minister, or
    c. family counseling service.
    (Look under "Family Counseling Services" or "Mental Health" in the Yellow Pages or the first few pages of telephone book.)
3. Relate symptoms and problem to intake worker. Indicate that it is an emergency; or make an appointment for outpatient treatment.
4. In extreme emergency, go to the emergency room of the nearest hospital.

Bibliography

Crewdson, John. *By Silence Betrayed*. New York: Harper & Row, 1988.

DePaulo, J. Raymond, Jr., and Ablow, Keith Russell. *How to Cope with Depression*. New York: McGraw-Hill, 1989.

Elkind, David. *The Hurried Child*. Boston: Addison-Wesley Publishing Co., 1981.

Engel, Beverly. *The Right to Innocence*. New York: Ivy Books, 1989.

Esser, Dr. Aristide, and Lacey, Sylvia. *Mental Illness: A Home Care Guide*. New York: John Wiley & Sons, 1989.

Forward, Susan, and Buck, Craig. *Betrayal of Innocence. Incest and Its Devastation*. New York: Penguin Books, 1978.

Meeks, John, MD. *High Times/Low Times. How to Cope with Teenage Depression*. PIA Press, 1988.

Minn, W. *Children Without Childhood*. New York: Viking Penguin Press, Inc., 1987.

Napier, Augustus, with Carl Whitaker. *The Family Crucible*. New York: Harper & Row, 1978.

Rapoport, Judith, MD. *The Boy Who Couldn't Stop Washing*. New York: E.P. Dutton, 1989.

Rosenberg, Ellen. *Growing Up Feeling Good*. New York: Beaufort Books, Inc., 1983.

Samenow, Stanton, PhD. *Before It's Too Late*. New York: Times Books, 1989.

———. *Inside the Criminal Mind*. New York: Times Books, 1984.

Sheehan, David, MD. *The Anxiety Disease*. New York: Bantam Books, 1983.

Valette, Brett. *A Parent's Guide to Eating Disorders*. New York:

Avon Books, 1988.
Weinberg, George. *The Heart of Psychotherapy*. New York: St. Martin's Press, 1984.
Wender, Paul. *The Hyperactive Child, Adolescent, and Adult*. New York: Oxford University Press, 1987.

Index